Transferable
Skills in Higher
Education

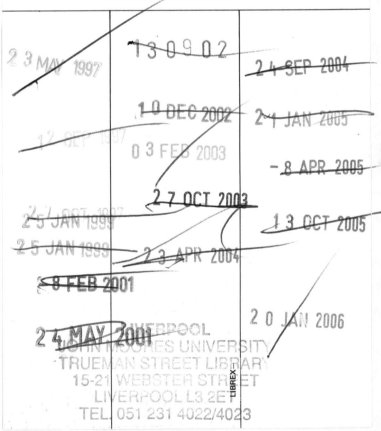

Transferable Skills in Higher Education

EDITED BY

Alison Assiter

**KOGAN
PAGE**

London • Philadelphia

First published in 1995

Kogan Page Limited
Pentonville Road
London N1 9JN

British Library Cataloguing in Publication Data

A CIP record for this book is available from the British Library.

ISBN 0 7494 1550 9

Typeset by Photoprint, Torquay
Printed and bound in Great Britain by
Biddles Ltd, Guildford and King's Lynn.

Contents

Foreword

Harold Silver

We have only just begun to confront what it means for a higher education to be 'student centred'. The concept has until recently been generally interpreted (when not ignored or rejected) to mean a new strategy for helping students through an old rite of passage. Student constituencies have been recognised in the great majority of institutions as already or potentially much less homogeneous, but students have still been perceived mainly as 'recipients', making a scheduled journey through a curriculum, even where the degree of choice in the curriculum has increased. Student centring the experience of the curriculum (the rite of passage) has been seen as easing adjustment to it by a variety of teaching strategies and student feedback mechanisms. A more fundamental reinterpretation is not, or not just, related to customer rights or an even more learner-friendly 'delivery' of the curriculum. It has more to do with situating the higher education experience in a continuum of experience and need, including pre-entry expectations and preparation, and the anticipation of outcomes and the uses of a higher education – including, but not only, employment.

There is, of course, a long tradition of defining education as 'an active continuous process of cooperation between teacher and learner'.[1] In spite of the determined efforts of generations of proponents, however, the implementation of such a process has been weak or short lived. Of the various considerations now involved in the interpretation of the notion of 'student centred', three are of prime importance: definitions of what it means to be a 'student', definitions of the nature and purposes of a 'curriculum', and the interaction of the two. The changing student constituency coincides with changing perceptions and self-perceptions of students. An American study of higher education and the expectations of the partners ended by stressing that 'responsibility in a learning institution is a two-way street', and described students as 'the workers in the educational process'.[2] The two-way street in Britain has become more and more denizened with people of a kind once excluded from entry – older, diversified by race and gender, recommended by their prior experiential learning, part time, transferring credit and so on. The street is, in fact, more than two-way, since there are changed pressures and

1

expectations on the university which affect the internal relationship – charters, funding mechanisms, quality scrutiny, the interests of employers and a variety of publics. Although the concept of 'workers in the educational process' rightly underlines the participation of these and more traditional students in 'the process', it is more helpful to describe them as co-workers in the making of education. The definition is more useful than that of customer or consumer or client, who buy services but don't make them. The student in 'student centred' is, even if a recipient in a two-way process, also a maker.

The curriculum has been traditionally a self-contained rite. It remains so in institutions committed to discipline-based degrees, though in these cases choice and action learning may be elements in their adaptation to new circumstances. The traditional view of the curriculum has been knowledge based, and the student seen as apprentice or customer has been given or helped to acquire, in one view described by Oakeshott, a collection of skills which constitute the 'inheritance of human accomplishments – which we may call a civilisation'. Acquiring one of these skills, 'that of a lawyer, a doctor, an accountant, a farmer or a commercial traveller – is taking possession of a part of this inheritance of human achievement in a process of learning'.[3] Even in this view, however, the curriculum has widely collapsed. In some cases there have been attempts to create a 'learner-centred' curriculum, but the very restructuring of the curriculum in modular and interdisciplinary ways has often resulted in greater student control over their programmes, and what some people have called their 'empowerment'. In both the packaging of learning opportunities and in emphases on competences, abilities, outcomes and strategies of work-based and other approaches to learning, the meaning of a curriculum has therefore profoundly changed. Oakeshott's list of occupations, 30 years old, no longer fits many students' perceptions of the market, and the taxonomy of employments contains both such tightly defined destinies and the range of employment possibilities for which precise knowledge content is often irrelevant. The interest in skills, and especially in transferable skills, stems therefore not purely from changes in student constituencies, and in curriculum structure and choice, but also from the intangibles of the employment and other destinations to which the learning process points.

Approaches to learning which focus on concepts of skills or competences, as Len Holmes points out in Chapter 2, are modified by a range of adjectives. The assumptions can be widely divergent, and the implications of occupational or personal skills, professional competences or student capability may be very different. National Vocational Qualifications (NVQs) aim to meet 'national standards of occupational competence'; the Royal Society seeks the transmission of 'a coherent body of knowledge', the development of its 'conceptual understanding and application' – students would also 'benefit greatly from the development of a range of personal skills'; and Eraut points out that research into 'generic competence presents a complete contrast' to behaviourist versions of competency-based training.[4] These are just pointers to a considerable debate about skills and competences,[5] and curricula and teaching approaches depend on definitions. As many institutions have discovered, interpreting curricula and teaching in terms of skills and outcomes, while weighing the meaning of 'coherent bodies of know-ledge', may be a complex and protracted operation.

Institutions have, however, carefully navigated some of these difficult-ies, often within the subjects which remain the basis of curricula and with Enterprise in Higher Education (EHE) or other support for the exploration of transferable skills. At the University of Plymouth one of many developments in this area is a transferable skills programme in the Department of Geographical Sciences where group work skills have been addressed as part of the learning process. It is emphasised to students that 'the ability to work with other people in a team is an especially valuable life skill'. Past experience of working in groups relates to present student needs and 'after graduation in your professional life you will frequently be expected to participate as a team member or leader'. The department therefore has a strategy for helping students themselves to prepare for 'life after finals', and group work is both a present emphasis of the department and an implication for the future.[6] It has been easy, as Alison Assiter points out in Chapter 1, to misrepresent skills and competences as necessarily 'low-level and mechanical attributes', but there is now considerable experience of demonstrating that a skill-based, student-centred approach to learning can be neither hollow of content nor disruptive of the 'inheritance of human accomplishments'. The Royal Society's discussion concludes that the emphasis on skills 'should not depend on the programme of study chosen by the student . . . but should be a central part of higher education'.[7]

The direction taken by an institution like the University of North London, as reflected in this book, is therefore not an aberration. The attempt is to reinterpret the purpose of the university and the nature of a student-centred education through a focus on transferable skills and outcomes as an element in the continuity of the student's experience. As is clear from the contributions to the book, this is not to *undermine* the 'subject' focus in history or science or interior design or business studies. The development of a focus on transferable skills or student profiles or both is emphasised, in history for example, as a search for oral competence, the skills of quantitative analysis, student pride and satisfaction in what is achieved through oral interviews. There is emphasis on a variety of approaches to active learning, and in social science the importance in a university of not just acquiring knowledge, but of understanding the use of knowledge, through a process of reflexive learning. The portfolio developed in interior design as a result of sustained negotiation with professional designers acts as a bridge between education and the workplace. Students are placed in a position to identify the skills they need, develop them and to monitor the development. As Paul Corrigan and colleagues point out, it is possible in these ways to evade the pursuit of competences entirely for the functional requirements of occupations, and to pursue a 'more humanistic concern with developing skilled and purposeful individuals' – this latter being one outcome of EHE programmes. Discussions with employers in publishing, the leisure industry, oil refining, design, the civil service and elsewhere, who take students from the University of North London either for placements or for project research, or who themselves contribute to the programmes in English or chemistry or business studies, suggest that employment-related outcomes can themselves be 'humanistic'. Students are described by such employers as better able to communicate, more sure of what they can and wish to contribute as well as what they can learn and more able to work in a team.

The purposes with which the university, then the Polytechnic of North London (PNL), set out in 1991 – in terms not unlike those of other institutions defining the objectives of their EHE programmes – included auditing the competence elements of its programmes, the piloting of personal competence profiles and providing students with the opportunity 'to define the generic and course-specific competences they have attained through prior learning and experience and through their PNL courses of study'.[8] The projects by which these purposes were to be attained included, in the first year, work on a competence framework (in business and finance), personal competence profiling (in social science, film studies, computing and life sciences), the development of communication skills (for lawyers) and professional skills (for architects), as well as oral history recording skills (in history and Irish studies) and work-based learning in publishing (in English). Here, as in other institutions, the focus was on reviewing processes, piloting and developing approaches, and confronting implications for teaching, learning and assessment. The university had placed these explorations in the context of its mission to develop access to higher education, and adapted to embrace access to employment. The diversity of these projects was continued in that of the projects relating to skills and profiles over the later years of the EHE programme. The very diversity of the approaches, within an overall perspective of access to higher education and employment, reaching into the curriculum, methods of learning and teaching, assessment and educational support and guidance, is one of the most important features of the programme. It is important because we are still only beginning to understand the diversity of student needs, and the implications of pursuing strategies which place not just student development, but student-centred or student-controlled development, at the centre of the diagram.

It is essential, therefore, in considering the reports and analyses of the kind in this book, the discussions of transferable skills, profiles and the curriculum, to emphasise the process of which the higher education experience is a part. The process has changed for all students, but there is particular interest in an institution like North London in the fact that the majority of entrants to higher education are now 'mature', older or adult students. The university student body is 'multiracial and predominantly mature',[9] but the changing composition of the student body in most of higher education presents the same implications. A report which specifically addresses these implications relates them to the development of a higher education and the lifelong process of which it is a part, and includes an emphasis on skills and their meanings:

'A part of the entitlement to higher education will be support to develop and maintain the qualities and skills needed for lifelong independent learning. These will include the explicit development of core and study skills, personal transferable skills, decision making and planning skills and knowledge of sources of support and information. The aim will be to strengthen each individual's ability to integrate their own practice in paid and unpaid work and learning.'[10]

Experience of the explicit pursuit of communication and presentation, group effort and the strategies of problem solving are no less valuable as liberal education for having purpose.

These and other emphases on competence, outcomes or transferable skills are capable of distortion, and of embodiment in narrow, poor, illiberal curricula and pedagogy, and a distortion of the meaning of 'student centred'. But, as every history of education demonstrates, this has sometimes or mainly been true of classics, modern languages, mathematics, science, medicine or law, at all their levels and in all institutions. Much of the literature on higher education is about the struggle to know but, as this book illustrates, knowing is also about the application and use of knowledge. The opportunity for students to develop the kinds of skills under discussion here is integral to the struggle to know, an enhancement of the context and content of discovery. It is possible to incorporate the curricular, learning and teaching dimensions of an institution into a process which takes account of the life of the student before and after, as well as within, the experience of higher education, and gives meaning to a student-centred mission. Such a direction is towards a new interpretation also of the meaning of an academic community. A defence of the basis of the developments discussed in this book is a defence of liberal values responding to new conditions and ideas, but particularly to the centrality of students in the definition of the purposes and processes involved. Skills are not given, they are coproduced.

Notes

1. Greenall, S (1971) 'Student views on wastage', *Universities Quarterly*, 25, 2, p. 138.
2. Wingspread Group on Higher Education (1993) *An American Imperative: Higher Expectations for Higher Education*, Wingspread Group, University of Wisconsin, Milwaukee, p. 16.
3. Michael J Oakeshott (1967) 'The definition of a university', *The Journal of Educational Thought*, 1, 3, p. 6.
4. National Council for Vocational Qualifications (NCVQ) (nd) *The National Council for Vocational Qualifications . . . Its Purposes and Aims*, NCVQ, London, p. 6; Royal Society Study Group (1993) *Higher Education Futures*, Royal Society, London, p. 5; Eraut, M (1994) *Developing Professional Knowledge and Competence*, Falmer, London, pp. 169–72.
5. For two widely different approaches to the debate see Winter, R (1992) ' "Quality management" or "the educative workplace": Alternative visions of competence-based education', *Journal of Further and Higher Education*, 16, 3, pp. 100–115, and Barnett, R (1994) *The Limits of Competence*, Society for Research in Higher Education and Open University Press, Buckingham.
6. Chalkley, B. (nd) *Transferable Skills Programme: Group Work*, Department of Geographical Sciences and Enterprise in Higher Education, University of Plymouth.
7. Royal Society (1993) *Higher Education Futures*, p. 25.
8. Polytechnic of North London (1991) *PNL Enterprise in Higher Education: Annex 1*, PNL, London, p. 1.
9. University of North London (1994) *Annual EHE Report*, UNL, London, p. 1.
10. National Institute of Adult Continuing Education (1993) *An Adult Higher Education: a vision*, NIACE, Leicester, p. 34.

Section One:

Transferable Skills and the Enterprise in Higher Education (EHE) Programme

In 1963 Robbins defined the aims of higher education (HE) as follows:

- instruction in skills suitable to play a part in the division of labour;
- promotion of the general powers of the mind;
- the advancement of learning;
- the transmission of a common culture and common standards.

The Council for National Academic Awards' (CNAA) Principle 3, developed a little later, stated that the aims of an HE programme should include 'the development of the students' intellectual and imaginative powers; their understanding and judgement; their problem-solving skills; their ability to communicate; their ability to see relationships within what they have learned' (CNAA, 1989). This version of the principle was based on earlier variants.

Twenty years ago Noel Entwistle surveyed academic staff at his own institution, Edinburgh University. He asked them what the point of their activities was. Their replies were as follows:

'More recently I've come . . . to the view that economists have acquired a way of looking at the world which is indelible, and even though they may not find themselves in a position where they can use their analytical techniques, in fact their whole way of treating questions is affected by this kind of training.'

A second, a philosopher, said:

'a philosophical approach should bring out and develop the ability to approach questions analytically.'

A lecturer in physics described his approach:

'We want to develop certain skills in the laboratory . . . the ability to design the apparatus necessary to carry out the particular experiments . . . to interpret the numbers . . . to develop mathematical and deductive skills.'

This particular individual did go on to say:

'Thirdly, we want – perhaps too much – to cover the entire ground of classical and modern physics so that they have a fairly comprehensive idea of what the entire corpus of knowledge is in the subject.'

At least the lecturer recognised that this is 'perhaps too much'. 'Other lecturers were more critical of the value of pure subject knowledge. Here is one:

'Most of one's time one is enslaving [the student] to certain techniques and disciplines in order that he·[sic] shall be accepted as an exponent of that sort of discipline.'

But the unifying theme in all responses was the desire to enable the development of *critical thinking* skills. (From Entwistle et al. 1984.)

At that time there appeared to be little controversy about skills development in HE. Since then, however, the concept of 'skill' has come into sharper focus. Some have argued, indeed, that the term has been corrupted by its association with initiatives which are perceived to be employer driven. In fact, recently a certain amount of scepticism as been expressed about the concept of a 'transferable skill'. This first – more theoretical – section of the book outlines some of the recent critiques of the concept of 'transferable skill' and offers a range of responses to them. My own chapter develops a response to the specific form of scepticism outlined by Ron Barnett in his recent book, *The Limits of Competence*. Paul Corrigan et al. defend a 'modernist' conception of the university against both 'pre-modern' and postmodern critiques; and Len Holmes rejects what he calls 'positivist' readings of the concept of 'transferable skill' in favour of an approach he calls 'social-discursive'. Instead of seeing a skill as an 'entity', he argues, we ought to be viewing the concept as a 'means of helping students articulate their claims to be able to do the kinds of activities which are conventionally expected of those who are highly educated' (Holmes, Chapter 2). Each of the three chapters represents an argument to the effect that the concept of a 'transferable skill' is useful and valuable.

There are two additional chapters in this first section of the book – one on support for staff in the development of skills (Chapter 4) and the other on the student tutoring scheme (Chapter 5) – each of which sets out to facilitate the development of particular kinds of skill. Although neither of these chapters sets out, as do the other three, to respond to a sceptic about skills, each constitutes, in its own way, an indirect response to such a sceptic.

References

Barnett, Ron (1994) *The Limits of Competence*, Society for Research in Higher Education and Open University Press, Buckingham.

Council for National Academic Awards (1989) *Handbook*, CNAA, London.

Entwistle, Noel, Hounsell, Dai and Marton, Terence (eds) (1984) *The Experience of Learning*, Scottish Academic Press, Edinburgh.

Robbins, Lord (1963) *The Robbins Report on HE*, Report of the Committee, HMSO, London.

Chapter 1

Transferable Skills: A Response to the Sceptics

Alison Assiter

Background

In the 1980s, a number of surveys were conducted which suggested that graduates in the UK were underequipped for employment. Surveys of employer satisfaction with the abilities of their graduate employees indicated skills shortages in the following areas: giving oral presentations, written communication, numeracy and IT abilities (Roizen and Jepson, 1985; Brennan and McGeever, 1987).

Following these surveys the government, through a number of White Papers (*Working Together*, HMSO, 1986; *Higher Education: Meeting the Challenge*, HMSO, 1987; *Higher Education: A New Framework*, HMSO, 1991), set out to increase or improve the links between education in general, and higher education (HE) in particular, and employment. Some of the arguments of these papers were couched in terms of the need for labour mobility, both within and between sectors, in an economy driven by technological innovation and commercial competition (BTEC, 1991, p. 4). But the claim was also made that graduate jobs, anyway, require individuals who are flexible and adaptable. For example:

'The high-tech world is a fast-moving, ever-changing environment which needs people who have the capacity to learn and develop, to move and change with the

needs of the organisation: who are prepared to break the mould of the past' (Bailey, 1990, p. 71).

It has been argued, therefore, that government, students themselves and employers increasingly will expect an HE qualification to imply that skills have been acquired that can be transferred to employment (see, for example, Pearson and Pike, 1990; AGR, 1993).

Theorists of the HE process already notice a change in focus, away from pure knowledge acquisition, towards employment-related outcomes (Atkins et al., 1993; Barnett, 1994).

Two initiatives are noteworthy in this general context. One is the Royal Society for Arts (RSA) Education for Capability Initiative, whose original manifesto proclaimed that there is a serious imbalance in Britain today between 'education' and 'training'. It went on to argue that this imbalance is harmful to individuals, to industry and, more generally, to society. A well-balanced education, the RSA suggested, should include the 'exercise of critical skills, the competence to undertake and complete tasks and the ability to cope with everyday life; and also doing all these things in cooperation with others' (RSA, 1991, p. 5). The other programme – Enterprise in Higher Education (EHE) – encouraged the development of 'enterprising people', who are 'resourceful, adaptable, creative, innovative and dynamic' (Training Agency, 1989). Among the proposed definitions of 'enterprise' is the following – 'transferable skills: the generic capabilities which allow people to succeed in a wide range of different tasks and jobs' (Training Agency, 1990, p. 5).

The ethos of these initiatives has not, however, gone unchallenged. In this chapter I will outline some of these challenges and offer some responses. The challenges represent fears and worries on the part of many academics in HE, that higher education institutions may be changing for the worse. I hope to show that, at least as far as the focus on transferable skills is concerned, these fears are unfounded.

Skills: low-level and mechanical?

One argument that is often put forward about skills is that such things tend to be low-level, mechanical attributes. This not simply a philosophical debating point, but one which represents a genuine worry about the purpose of higher education; and it was put, twenty years ago, by Peters in the following way: there is an antithesis between the two sets of concepts: 'training, skills, narrowness of application, instrumental value', and 'education, knowledge, understanding, broad cognitive perspective and intrinsic value' (Peters, 1966). Sometimes this distinction is drawn in such a way as to encompass the broader distinction between 'training' on the one hand and 'education' on the other. Certainly, in the form in which it was put by an educational dualist like Minogue, writing in the early 1970s, it was deliberately intended to constitute a statement of the dualism between 'education' (the business of universities, at least, and maybe a few other seats of learning, like some schools) and 'training' (Minogue, 1973). As Minogue stated the distinction, it was one between academic inquiry and other forms of inquiry. Academic inquiry is *intellectual*; it is not concerned with practical matters. He argues that 'there is a consistent difference in the kind of meaning found in academic discourse, by contrast with that found in the world at large'. He explicitly rejects what he calls 'Monism'.

There are those, therefore, who have deliberately set out to proclaim that there is a fundamental distinction between HE institutions and the rest of society. Ron Barnett's work, I believe, represents a different, and more recent, version of this dualism, and it is expressed very differently from Minogue's. I will consider Barnett's view in a moment. However, there are those, and I frequently hear this view expressed in my own institution, who would want to break down the divide between 'education' and 'training', but who would wish to hang on to a distinction between 'skills' on the one hand, and 'knowledge' on the other. Those who put this view would argue that the language of 'education' versus 'training' is appropriate for an élite HE system, whose participants come from a small segment of classes 1 and 2, but not for a mass HE system which, theoretically at least, allows participation from wider segments of society. In wishing to retain the distinction between 'skills' and 'knowledge' they would argue that 'skills' talk is appropriate for those vocational training colleges where the 'lower' classes tended, and still tend, to congregate, but it is not the language of HE. In other words, they wish to retain Peters' dichotomy. There are problems, however, with any attempt to retain this distinction.

First of all it has been argued that, for example, 'problem-solving skills', 'management skills' or 'interpersonal skills' all rest upon considerable knowledge and understanding. The suggestion, therefore, implicit in Peters' classification system, that 'skills' are intrinsically different from 'knowledge' is undermined, at least in the case of these three types of skill. The second point that must be made is that psychologists, at least since Bloom, have tended to operate with a much broader definition of 'skill' than Peters' dichotomy implies. The commonplace, everyday use of the term 'skill' has tended to emphasise motor aspects of a task, such as wordprocessing or driving a car. However, there are several objections to so doing. On the one hand, psychologists have researched skills such as 'perceptive motor skills' or 'sensory skills', where these descriptors categorise cognitive abilities. On the other hand Bloom (1956) has devised a list of specifically 'cognitive' skills as follows: knowledge, interpretation, application, analysis, synthesis and evaluation. Bloom's particular taxonomy has been criticised, but we continue to see it argued that these types of skill are the business, even the 'core' business, of universities. If these cognitive skills exist, and are taken to be fundamental to HE, then once again, but from a different perspective, Peters' distinction between 'skills' and 'knowledge' is rendered questionable.

The point might be made that the kinds of skill usually identified in the EHE initiative, or in the writings of the Higher Education for Capability (HEC) Initiative, do not include Bloom's 'cognitive' abilities. The kinds of skill, for example, identified by the National Curriculum Council (NCC) as 'core' are the following:

- problem solving
- communication
- personal skills
- application of mathematics
- IT
- foreign language competence.

This list is broadly comparable to the set described by the Confederation of British Industry (CBI) and by the National Council for Vocational Qualifications (NCVQ) in its literature on 'Core Skills'. It is certainly true that it does not incorporate Bloom's 'analysis' or 'evaluation'. However, I have never heard it argued, even by the most die-hard of NCVQ sympathisers, that universities should *not* be in the business of teaching, or encouraging students to acquire, cognitive skills. Liberal academics, however, probably including Peters and Minogue, *have* argued that it is not the business of the university to teach skills, because skills *per se* are believed by them to be low level and routine.

HE: a changing culture?

The above argument is probably less important, however, than those put cogently by Barnett (1994) and in a slightly different form by Prickett (1994), that the culture of HE is changing, and changing for the worse as a result of moves like EHE and HEC and the statements of the body Council for Industry and Higher Education (CIHE). Barnett makes a number of points on this issue. He encapsulates what we are seeing in a move from:

'higher education → knowledge → society'   to

'society → knowledge → higher education'.

Barnett is sceptical about the value of this kind of shift in focus, including the not-so-hidden agenda of projects such as the EHE, to allow the market-place, or industry, to shape higher education programmes of study. Barnett suggests that, increasingly in HE, the state is identifying the forms of knowing and development it sees as worthwhile and communicating this to the universities, with the student's identity becoming predetermined to fulfil the instrumental ends of economic and social survival.

Another argument of this kind is put by Stephen Prickett (1994), who argues that there are two versions of EHE: a 'free market', Darwinian version, according to which academic subjects compete in the market-place for funding and students, and (presumably) those that survive will do so because they are the most responsive to the 'needs' of the market. A second version of EHE is more 'corporatist', and sets out to 'control' what goes on in the universities. Prickett concludes that EHE is inherently divided between these two notions and that it is, therefore, ultimately benign and non-threatening. Barnett, however, remains very worried about recent innovations in HE.

One point against the EHE programme, made by Barnett (p. 89), is that there may be an incompatibility between an individual's personal development and the development of qualities needed for survival in the world of work. Does Barnett's argument apply against the development of skills? The answer must be that it does not. If one were to take the strongest version of the argument and, for the moment, exclude Bloom's cognitive skills from the hypothetical list, it would sound odd indeed to argue that HE should not be concerned with the development of 'core' skills, on the grounds that it should not have anything to do with any initiative that may be market driven. I have yet to hear any academic arguing that HE should *not* be concerned with developing communication skills, problem-solving and information technology (IT) abilities. Many have argued that this should not be its core or its only business, but most academics, from most disciplines, when pressed to justify their pro-grammes for students who are not likely to become specialists in the academic's own discipline, have done so in terms of its fostering these kinds of development in those students. Indeed, it is interesting to note that even those who suggest, following Peters, that HE is concerned with 'knowledge' and *not* skills, would not actually deny, when pressed, that HE is concerned to develop communication and analytic abilities. 'Skills' would implicitly, for Peters et al., *exclude* those abilities. In other words, even if the 'core skills' agenda *is* market driven, it is very difficult for anyone to argue against it *also* being good for individual learning, for personal development and for life. It is difficult, therefore, taking Barnett's view and applying it to the issue of skills development, to see how core skills development *could* be incompatible with development for life.

There is a general liberal point which Barnett might argue is undermined by the above. This is J S Mill's point, in his submission to the Royal Commission of 1851, that true learning should be protected from the pressures of the market-place. This claim, however, can be interpreted in a number of different ways. If it means that learning should not be explicitly tied to the short-term profitability of 'the market' , one immediately comes up with the difficulty of determining which market or which company. Is it Rolls-Royce, Ford or Peugeot? Of course it could not be all three, and the absurdity of the claim, therefore, is apparent. In a competitive market it is logically impossible to have 'the market' determining the ends of HE. If Mill's claim is interpreted to mean that 'the market' should not determine what goes on in HE then, in a sense, he must be right because a pure free market cannot 'determine' anything. If Mill is taken to be arguing against the idea that universities should act as one group of competitors, in a competitive market, however, then the question might be raised: why should universities be exempt from the market? In a market system, what is special about universities, as opposed to shoe shops or publishing houses? There are major issues at stake here, and there are many in HE, including many sympathisers of the EHE programme, who would be unhappy to see HE lose its ability to engage in critical research or in the development of critical reasoning processes that may not serve the immediate short-term interests of any market. To this sense of Mill's point, therefore, I am sympathetic.

If Mill is interpreted, on the other hand, to be opposing the notion of the state determining what goes on in HE, he would, once again, have much support, from liberals and Marxists alike, and from me. The general point – that HE should be free to criticise accepted wisdoms, that it should encourage reflection upon common-sense attitudes, that it should be allowed to look to long-term goals – is at the core of academic freedom (for individual academics, at least). But there is another side to the argument, which is increasingly being put today by exponents of the EHE programme and others. This is that academics (like students), as well as having rights (to academic freedom, for example), also have responsibilities to their students. In a situation where 10 per cent of 18-year-olds graduated to guaranteed jobs in the professions, this responsibility could be exercised by them unconsciously. Academics exercised it just by doing their jobs as academics. But, in a situation where 30 per cent (in the UK) of 18-year-olds graduate, where the biggest growth in HE overall is in mature students and where those students are not guaranteed jobs in the professions or anywhere at all, this responsibility can no longer be exercised unconsciously. This is where transferable skills come in. Employers, from all sectors of the economy, argue that they need graduates with core skills. So, if Mill's point is interpreted to mean that academics have no responsibilities towards the futures of their students and therefore that the market, in this sense, should not interfere with HE, I would argue that he is wrong. This may well mean that Barnett's society → knowledge → HE is in one sense correct. However, I would argue further that the sort of causal (or other) connection represented by Barnett's arrows today is far less sinister than that represented by the church in medieval times. The ancient European universities were not founded to provide for the disinterested pursuit of learning but for the administrative needs both of the church and of the state. As Prickett points out,

'the trivium and the quadrivium at mediaeval Oxford were both practical. Grammar, rhetoric and logic were powerful tools for both administration and preaching, and an essential foundation for law and medicine.'

Prickett also comments on the more practical bias of the Scottish universities in the nineteenth century, 'whose scholarly supremacy over the English ones was widely acknowledged'. He describes how, in the 1800s, the young Lord Palmerston was sent first to Edinburgh University for four years to gain an education, and then to Cambridge to meet the right people (Prickett, p. 173).

Transferable skills: critical or instrumental reasoning

Here I'd like to return to the substantial point behind Barnett's critique of recent trends in HE. He argues that we are witnessing the beginnings of a triumph of Habermasian 'instrumental reasoning' in HE, as opposed to 'critical or evaluative' modes of thought. Instrumental reasoning, for Habermas, is that mode of reasoning which has to do with the prediction of the workings of the environment in which we find ourselves, which stems from an instrumental interest in those matters. There is another form of reasoning, according to Habermas, which by contrast is critical and evaluative, and which stems from what Habermas calls an 'emancipatory' interest – an interest which human beings have in comprehending the world and in freeing themselves from constraining forms of action. Marxism and Freudianism are, according to Habermas, the two central contenders for this type of thinking.

Barnett argues that there are a number of characteristics of the latter modes of reasoning – a concern for understanding, for wisdom and an interest in educational processes, as opposed to outcomes – that are integral to HE, and that are being undermined by initiatives like the EHE programme and an interest in transferable skills. Critical reasoning, according to him, is valuable because it stems from an interest in 'the truth' (p. 36). This, he suggests, is no longer the primary focus in HE. Its focus is becoming that of serving, instrumentally, the needs of the market, 'society' or 'the state'.

Barnett himself is interested primarily in the critical reasoning *process*. One might however ask questions, as others with an interest in pedagogy have done, about the context in which, for Habermas, critical reasoning can take place. Habermas' ideal of 'knowledge governed by an interest in emancipation' takes place in conditions that approximate to an 'ideal speech situation', a situation in which there is the greatest possible degree of autonomy and equality among those engaging in the 'speech situation'. Of course this ideal is not possible in an absolute sense in the university, where there is an intrinsic differentiation of status, knowledge and experience between the 'academic' and the student.

But the question one could ask is, which educational practices best approximate to that ideal? The answer, I contend, is that the practices of the EHE programme, with its focus on *student learning* and on the development of transferable skills in the student, more closely approximate to that ideal than approaches to HE which have academics transmitting *their* knowledge through lectures and silent seminars. For this is what, traditionally, many have done, rather than, as Barnett suggests, sharing with their students a desire to discover 'the truth'. Indeed, students who are encouraged to communicate and to solve problems for themselves are more likely to challenge the academics' version of 'the truth' than those who are more compliant and more submissive. The teaching of transferable skills, then, can have a positive effect on the discovery of 'the truth' and it is, in fact, more likely to approximate to the conditions under which Habermasian 'critical reasoning' can develop, than an approach which has academics disseminating their 'knowledge' to a passive group of students. Additionally, it has an effect on the student's ability to learn and on her ability to function in life outside the university. Far from the EHE programme undermining the development of critical reasoning, therefore, I would argue that it is more likely to foster its development, by encouraging a focus on how students learn, than earlier academic traditions which give less scope to students to challenge received forms of wisdom.

Barnett regrets the loss of critical emancipatory thinking by recent innovations like EHE. As a graduate of philosophy, I should be one of the first to be up on the liberal barricades with him if I thought that critical reason was under threat, but I do not believe that EHE and the recent focus on transferable skills is doing that at all. On the contrary, I believe that it has the potential to do precisely the opposite.

References

Association of Graduate Recruiters (AGR) (1993) *Graduate Employment Prospects*, Association of Graduate Careers Advisors (AGCAS), London.

Atkins, M, Beattie, J and WB Dockrell (1993) *Assessment Issues in Higher Education*, Sheffield, Sheffield Employment Department.

Bailey, A (1990) 'Personal transferable skills for employment: the role of higher education' (1994), in Wright, P (ed), *Industry and Higher Education*, Society of Research in Higher Education (SRHE) and Open University Press, Buckingham.

Barnett, R (1994) *The Limits of Competence*, SRHE and Open University Press, Buckingham.

Bloom, R S (ed) (1956) *Taxonomy of Educational Objectives Handbook, 1: Cognitive Domain*, McKay, New York.

Brennan, J and McGeever, P (1987) *CNAA Graduates: Their Employment and Their Experiences after College*, CNAA Development Services, no 13.

BTEC (1991) *Common Skills*, BTEC, London.

HMSO (1986) *Working Together* DE/DES, London.

HMSO (1987) *Higher Education: Meeting the Challenge*, DE/DES, London.

Minogue, K (1973) *The Concept of the University*, Weidenfeld & Nicolson, London.

NCC, *The Whole Curriculum*, Guidance 3, York, NCC, 1990.

Pearson, R and Pike, G (1990) *The IMS Graduate Review*, The Institute of Management Studies (IMS), Brighton, 1990

Peters, R S (1966) *Ethics and Education*, Allen & Unwin, London.

Prickett, S (1994) 'EHE: nice work, or ivory tower *v* exchange and mart', *HE Quarterly* 48, 3, July.

RSA (1991) *Education for Capability*, London.

Roizen, J and Jepson, M (1985) *Degrees for Jobs: Employer expectations of HE*, SRHE/NFER – Nelson, Guildford.

TA (1990) *Enterprise in Higher Education: Key features of EHE proposals*, Employment Department, Moorfoot, Sheffield.

Chapter 2

Skills: A Social Perspective
Len Holmes

The irresistible rise of transferable skills?

There does indeed appear to be some quality of irresistibility about the increasing attention being paid to the notion that higher education can and should enable students to develop abilities which are in some way transferable to contexts separate from the subject discipline studied. Over a decade ago, the old NAB (National Advisory Board for Public Sector Higher Education) and the University Grants Committee (UGC) endorsed such a view in a joint statement: 'The abilities most valued in industrial, commercial and professional life as well as in public and social administration are the transferable intellectual and social skills.' (NAB/UGC, 1984).

A variety of terms is used to refer to apparently similar abilities. Usually the term 'skill' (or sometimes 'competence' or 'competency') is prefaced by 'personal' and/or 'transferable'. There is also, of course, the term 'capability', as used by the Higher Education for Capability Initiative (Stephenson and Weil, 1992), and the expression 'enterprise skills', as originally used in the Enterprise in Higher Education Initiative. Whatever term is used, the *explicit* message is clear: these abilities are important to society and to the individual, and should therefore figure prominently in the curriculum. 'A higher education system which provides its students with these skills is serving society well' (ibid.).

Views (supportive and oppositional) about the supposed need for relevance of higher education to the world outside the academy are not new. In particular, arguments about the extent to which higher education should be separate from the 'practical' affairs of industry and commerce have continued since the nineteenth century (see, for example, Silver and Brennan, 1988; Barnett, 1990). Certainly employers and graduates alike have, in reality, taken it for granted that there are certain general abilities gained through higher education which are useful and of value in employment. Moreover, there seems to be little evidence that academics have been vociferous in denying this.

What is new in the recent rise to prominence of the notion of 'transferable skills' and the like, is the attempt to place these more centrally within the curriculum. No longer are students assumed to be developing such abilities, almost incidentally to the subject-specific learning. Rather, novel approaches to teaching and assessment are to be used, whereby explicit attention is paid to the supposed transferable skills. Indeed, 'teaching' itself becomes a term to avoid, as the emphasis shifts to notions of learning through 'experience', especially in 'real world' settings. In respect of assessment, we have seen the rise of 'profiles' and 'portfolios' which are deemed to provide more meaningful accounts of a student's abilities than overall course grades and degree classifications.

The context of higher education

Such developments do, of course, have to be seen within the wider context. Conservative government policies, and the policies of the opposition parties, have emphasised the perceived need for education to help improve the performance of the UK's economy. Structural changes in higher education, particular the massive increase in student numbers without a proportionate increase in resources, have put great pressure not only on academic and administrative staff but also the systems which they operate. In addition there have been major structural changes in graduate employment patterns, along with high levels of debt with which students graduate. These and other factors combine in lending support to those who argue that institutions of higher education should change their curricula to meet more explicitly the needs of employers and therefore of students seeking jobs and careers on the basis of their higher education.

Such conventional employment-related justification for transferable skills has been clearly and cogently demolished by Gubbay (1994). Moreover, even if such skills were required by employers, it does not follow that universities should help students to develop them and assess students in respect of them. After all, universities are not surrogate employment and training agencies. However, it does appear that the rhetoric adopted in promoting notions of higher education being (at least in part) preparation for employment does serve to persuade many of the need for developing and assessing 'personal' or 'transferable skills'.

Searching for 'transferable skills'

A variety of initiatives in higher education have involved some form of search for these supposed abilities, by whatever term they are called. Lists and models abound, of greater or lesser length and complexity. NAB and UGC expressed them in simple terms: 'The personal or non-academic skills of students, which higher education is expected to develop, include the general communication, problem-solving, teamwork and inter-personal skills required in employment' (NAB/UGC, 1986, p. 3).

In a study of employers' stated perceptions of the 'transferable employment skills' needed by graduates, a list of 20 such 'skills' was produced (Smith et al., 1989). A project by Nankivell and Shoolbred at Birmingham Polytechnic on staff perceptions of 'personal transferable skills' was based on the view that 'there is a general consensus on the major groups of skills – written and oral skills, interpersonal and teamwork skills, problem-solving skills and information handling skills' (Drew et al., 1992, p. 11). Drew's report, in the same paper published by the Standing Conference on Educational Development, concerned students' perceptions of 'personal skills and qualities' (PSQ), as identified in a project at Sheffield City Polytechnic. She states that it was decided not to specify PSQ, regarding this as unhelpful because 'different PSQ seemed relevant to different subject areas and individuals . . . It seemed more helpful to encourage staff and students to themselves identify relevant PSQ' (p. 39).

An action research project at Sheffield University led to a list of 108 'skills', which were placed into eight categories. This was later refined to produce a model which was intended to represent how these 'skills' related to 'zones', in terms of increasing complexity (Allen, 1993).

I shall return to the issue of the variety of such schema, but at this point it is important to recognise the positivist notions underlying these searches. The 'skills' are treated as having some independent reality, capable (in principle) of being identified and of being causally related to performance in a variety of settings. Once they have been identified generally they can be identified in particular individuals; ie individuals can be assessed to determine the extent to which they possess such abilities. Find some way of measuring these abilities and you then have a way of recording students' transferable skills, to include on some form of profile or transcript.

The positivist tendency in this area may also be seen in the broader area of competence-based education and training. There is now a considerable body of critical literature in that area, focusing particularly on flaws arising from the underlying positivism (eg, Ashworth and Saxton, 1990; Jacobs, 1990; Marsh and Holmes, 1990; Marshall, 1991; Stewart and Hamlin, 1992; Holmes, 1993; Assiter, 1993). Many of those critical views apply also in respect of transferable skills. Moreover, it does seem to be a rather naive positivism, with no attempt to engage in the rigorous hypothetico-deductive methodology normally adopted in positivist psychological studies. This would treat transferable skills as 'hypothetical constructs', taken as theoretical explanatory variables whose meaning is related to observable phenomena (and subject to empirical testing) rather than presumed entities in some non-observable domain (eg, the 'mind') (Harré and Gillett, 1994).

The lists of supposed skills tend to consist of a varied mix of different *sorts of things*, including 'personal qualities', 'values', particular 'skills' as well as the ability to 'apply knowledge and understanding'. Quite how these differ from each other, and how they can, if different *sorts of things*, be linked together as similar (ie, all 'transferable skills'), is not explained. Nor is explanation provided on how these 'transferable skills' give rise to (cause?) performance. Nor is there an explanatory theory of the contexts or domains within which 'transfer' supposedly takes place (Bridges, 1992). There are, then, serious problems with current formulations.

Rethinking transferable skills

In their review of the language used by employers in talking about the skills of managers, Hirsh and Bevan (1988) concluded that, while there was evidence of an emerging single language, this 'exists in terms of common words but not in terms of meaning' (p. 78). Earlier, Mangham and Silver (1986) had lamented the poverty of the language of managerial abilities, which impeded employer commitment to management training. Both pairs of researchers appear to assume that more precision in the terminology was both desirable and achievable. However, this may be an assumption worth questioning, particularly in the light of recent scholarship in the social and human sciences which seriously considers language use (eg, Potter and Wetherell, 1987; Shotter and Gergen, 1989; Burkitt, 1991; Edwards and Potter, 1992; Harré and Gillett, 1994).

The representational or 'picture' theory of language has been long discredited. This view regards the main use of language as that of representing, through symbolic forms, relationships between entities in the world. Thus most significant utterances were either true or false, depending upon whether or not the representation of circumstances in the world was accurate. Such truth or falsity could be tested empirically, by observing the circumstances held to be represented. The extreme form of this view was embodied in the verification principle of Logical Positivism.

Those utterances which were not, in principle, capable of such testing could not be regarded as factual, but *merely* expressive. So, at a stroke, all moral and metaphysical statements were rendered as incapable of being true or false; they were pseudo-statements, *mere* expressions of feelings or preferences.

The philosopher J L Austin effectively demolished such a simplistic view of the nature of language by pointing out that it is essentially a social practice. That is, we do things with words, such as promising, thanking, apologising, congratulating, approving. Thus

'many specially perplexing statements do not serve to indicate some specially odd additional feature of the reality reported, but to indicate (not to report) the circumstances in which the statement is made or reservations to which it is subject or the way it is to be taken and the like' (Austin, 1962, p. 3).

Taking this view, we might then consider whether 'specially perplexing statements', such as those concerned with abilities deemed to be necessary for performance, are *not* statements about causal connections in the world or descriptions of people. Rather, they are the basis on which we claim 'reasonableness' in the way we take decisions about granting or withholding credits, qualifications, jobs, and so on (Holmes, 1993; Holmes and Joyce, 1993).

If we consider how such terms as 'competence' and 'skill' have practical usefulness, it is clear that this arises from their future reference. That is, we judge that someone's future performance (of some tightly or loosely specified kind) will be as we would desire it, and so take some action or make some decision on the basis of that judgement. Such judgements are, of course, often made on the basis of evidence we have of past performance. However, such past performance would usually pass unremarked except in respect of what we believe it enables us to infer about future performance. That is, competence inferred is greater than performance observed (Holmes and Joyce, 1993).

Being future oriented, these judgements are inherently subject to the risk of being wrong. Moreover, an important aspect of such decisions and actions is that they are made in social settings, such that their consequences are borne not just by those taking them. So, for example, in recruiting graduates, a selection panel will appoint certain individuals who will then work for particular managers who were not involved in the recruitment process. In order to maintain confidence in their recruitment decisions, and to assure continued involvement in the process, the recruiters will seek to account for their choices in ways that are accepted as reasonable. Thus the language used to refer to the supposed characteristics of the candidates, on which choices were made, may be seen as 'conventions of warrant' (Gergen, 1989), ie discursive accounts of action that are socially legitimate. Indeed, the whole chain of processes linking assessment activities in educational settings, from the inscription of some 'verdict' (eg, class of degree awarded) on the individual, to the use of such verdicts for other purposes such as recruitment, may be seen as 'conventions of assessment' whereby the various links in the chain are warranted (Holmes, 1994).

A social view of skill and transfer

By rejecting the positivist assumptions within traditional approaches to transferable skills, it is therefore possible to develop an alternative, social-discursive approach. Under such a view both the notion of 'skill' and that of 'transfer' change. Now they become part of the language in which the key parties to the education–employment nexus can engage with each other. Those key parties particularly include students/graduates, employers and teachers. Employers can use the skills language to express what it is they are seeking in graduate recruits. Indeed, to some extent, the notion of 'transferable skills' has enabled employers, or at least certainly those claiming to speak on their behalf, to express dissatisfaction with what graduates could do. Such a claim, whatever its validity and its significance for *education*, has certainly been a powerful aspect of the rhetoric supporting policies for change.

Rather than engaging in a strategy of resistance to the skills agenda, educators may attempt to use the language to positive effect in two ways. First, they can build the case for continued and expanded resources from society, through the state, for higher education, by articulating more clearly the claim that it does indeed enable students to develop these prized skills. Secondly, students may be helped to use the skills language to articulate what they can do, and what they have done, in a way that is, reportedly, understood by employers. Both of these require an appropriation of the language, from its use in the call for change on the part of higher education to its use in asserting the value of higher education to society.

The notion of 'transfer' also changes in this approach. No longer is this seen as some process by which the graduate transfers some purported ability from an academic context to the employment setting. Rather, those who are engaged in decisions (on awarding qualifications or in recruitment) 'transfer' the warrant, endorsing as 'good' past performance and taking this as a reasonable basis for inferring that future performance in a different setting will be 'good'. The vocabulary used to describe both past and anticipated performance is a common one.

It is important that such a view of the language of transferable skills is not mistaken for the pseudo-precise conceptual classification system which positivist approaches would adopt. It is, rather, to be seen as a *normal* form of language. As such, it is imprecise and 'fuzzy', whereby meaning is not fixed in advance but negotiated through the responsive nature of engagement between the parties involved. It is no different from other aspects of social reality, which is, as Shotter (1993) argues, conversational. Normal language is rich in potential meanings, rather than a limited set of specific, precise terms. No wonder that those attempting to produce some standard list of skills terms have found such variety in the language actually used, as noted above. Not only is this to be expected, it is essential if the language of skills is to be of value.

Once we drop the misleading idea that we can achieve some precise definition of a specific set of transferable skills which will be of use in the manner desired, we can also drop the notion that we must find some methods for assessing students on these supposed abilities. Rather, the task now turns to one of helping students to *articulate their claims* to be able to do the kinds of activities which are conventionally expected of those who are highly educated. This involves developing their fluency in the appropriate languages, that of the immediate academic context as determined by the discipline being studied and that of the wider social context. It is through such language use that they can not only enhance their prospects in gaining access to desired employment but also act in an 'accountable' manner (see Shotter, 1989) when engaged in such employment.

This supports those approaches under initiatives such as Higher Education for Capability and Enterprise in Higher Education which attempt to develop *student-centred*, process-oriented forms of profiling, rather than *assessor-centred* (teacher or employer), product-oriented forms of records of achievement. Students need to engage in the use of the language of competence or transferable skills, through interaction and negotiation with others (and with themselves through the internal dialogue we call 'reflection'). They will not be helped by being 'branded' with some fixed, externally determined (and so counterfeit) measure of ability.

Of course some might, and have, objected that we can't allow students to lay claim to such abilities without checking that they're not lying, or exaggerating (or even underestimating themselves). This misses the whole point that the vocabulary of transferable skills is effectively meaningless unless the student is able to appropriate its use in their own experience, within the appropriate social ('conversational') contexts. This would involve the ability to justify any claim made to particular skills by pointing to the performances and activities through which they have been developed and/or exhibited. It would involve being able to negotiate the significance of such performances and activities with others, including their peers as well as tutors and prospective employers. The very nature of this social view denies any particular party any special gifts of insight into the 'reality' of students' abilities.

I am not claiming that this view of transferable skills, personal competence, etc, is itself without difficulties. We have to be alert to the way that changing language also changes the nature of the social reality which is in part constructed through language use (the 'order of things', to use Foucault's phrase). In my view, this emphasises the need for educators to engage with the transferable skills approach, to influence the direction it takes, rather than take a principled stance of maintaining 'purity' by disengagement. Under current and emerging political, economic and social conditions the meaning of higher education and its relationship to wider society is being remade. It seems clear that the notion of 'transferable skills' will form a key part in that remade meaning. The question is what meaning will be attached to the notion of transferable skills, and who will determine that meaning?

References

Allen, M (1993) *A Conceptual Model of Transferable Personal Skills*, Employment Department, Sheffield.

Ashworth, P and Saxton, J (1990) 'On "Competence" ', *Journal of Further and Higher Education* 14, 2, Summer.

Assiter, A (1993) 'Skills and knowledges: Epistemological models underpinning different approaches to teaching and learning', *Reflections in Higher Education*, 5, July, pp. 110–124.

Austin, J (1962) *How to Do Things with Words*, Clarendon Press, Oxford.

Barnett, R (1990) *The Idea of Higher Education*, Society for Research in Higher Education/Open University Press, Buckingham.

Bridges, D (1992) 'Transferable skills: A philosophical perspective', *Studies in Higher Education*, Summer.

Bridges, D (ed) (1994) *Transferable Skills in Higher Education*, University of East Anglia, Norwich

Burkitt, I (1991) *Social Selves*, Sage, London.

Drew, S, Nankivell, M and Shoolbred, M (1992) 'Personal skills – quality graduates', Standing Conference on Educational Development (SCED) Paper no 69.

Edwards, D and Potter, J (1992) *Discourse Psychology*, Sage, London.

Gergen, K (1989) 'Warranting voice and the elaboration of the self', in Shotter, J and Gergen, K (eds) *Texts of Identity*, Sage, London.

Gubbay, J (1994) 'A critique of conventional justifications for transferable skills', in Bridges, D (ed), *Transferable Skills in Higher Education*, University of East Anglia, Norwich.

Harré, R and Gillet, G (1994) *The Discursive Mind*, Sage, London.

Hirsh, W and Bevan, S (1988) *What Makes a Manager? In search of language for management skills*. Report 144, Institute of Manpower Studies, Brighton.

Holmes, L (1993) 'Talking of competence: How to rescue a useful concept', in *Papers from Innovations at the Crossroads – The Second Annual 'Innovations' Conference*, University College of North Wales, Bangor.

Holmes, L (1994) 'Is competence a "Confidence Trick"?', keynote address to the first Competence Network conference, University of Leicester, November.

Holmes, L and Joyce, P (1993) 'Rescuing the useful concept of managerial competence: From outcomes back to process', *Personnel Review*, 22, 6.

Jacobs, R (1990) 'No Simple Answers', in M Devine (ed.) *The Photofit Manager*, Unwin, London.

Mangham, I and Silver, M (1986) *Management Training: Context and Practice*, Economic and Social Research Council (ESRC).

Marsh, S and Holmes, L (1990) 'Dysfunctional analysis? A critical analysis of the "Standards in Training and Development"', paper presented to conference, 'A Qualified Success? Critical Perspectives on Competence-Based Education and Training', Polytechnic of North London, September.

Marshall, K (1991) 'NVQ's: An assessment of the "outcomes" approach to education and training', *Journal of Further and Higher Education*, 15, 3.

NAB/UGC (1984) *Higher Education and the Needs of Society* National Advisory Board for Public Sector Higher Education/University Grants Council, London.

NAB/UGC (1986) *Transferable Personal Skills in Employment: The Contribution of Higher Education*, National Advisory Board for Public Sector Higher Education/ University Grants Council, London.

Potter, J and Wetherell, M (1987) *Discourse and Social Psychology*, Sage, London.

Shotter, J (1989) 'Social accountability', in Shotter, J and Gergen, K (eds), *Texts of Identity*, Sage, London.

Shotter, J (1993) *Conversational Realities: Constructing life through language*, Sage, London.

Shotter, J and Gergen, K (eds) (1989) *Texts of Identity*, Sage, London.

Silver, H and Brennan, J (1988) *A Liberal Vocationalism*, Methuen, London.

Smith, D, Wolstencroft, T and Southern, J (1989) 'Personal Transferable Skills and the Job Demands on Graduates', *Journal of European Industrial Training*, 13, 8, pp. 25–31.

Stephenson, J and Weil, S (eds) (1992) *Quality in Learning: A capability approach in higher education*, Kogan Page, London.

Stewart, J and Hamlin, B (1992) 'Competence-based Qualifications: The case against change', *Journal of European Industrial Training*, 16, 7.

Chapter 3

A Modernist Perspective on Changes in the Higher Education Curriculum

Paul Corrigan, Mike Hayes and Paul Joyce

Introduction

In the 1980s the importance of competition and the market was the hallmark of many public policy initiatives. In the field of education academics found that educational qualifications were to face a new market entrant: the National Vocational Qualification (NVQ). This qualification did not require a learning process – it was based on industry-led notions of competence, it shunned the traditional pedagogic methods of educational institutions. According to NCVQ, candidates could be, indeed should be, assessed in the workplace by supervisors and managers with the required and certified competence in workplace assessment. So with the launch of NVQs a rival system of qualifications had been set up which many academics, and others, felt was implicitly an attack on the value of existing academic qualifications. But not every initiative was of this kind, and one at least was in keeping with the mood of the 1990s. The Enterprise in Higher Education (EHE) initiative matches well the 1990s

29

mood for partnership and the renewed appreciation of targeting for support and innovation those organisations and institutions that are established and have shown their durability. Equally, we can contrast the way in which NVQs put the emphasis on developing individuals to fit the functional requirements of occupations and the way in which the EHE initiative had a more humanistic concern with developing skilled and purposeful individuals. However, this is not an argument for the preference of the EHE initiative over NVQs; indeed there is a strong need to relate the development of functional competences and personal skills – each depends on the other. These issues are explored from within the perspective of higher education and with reference to the concerns and habits that filter higher education's responses to the EHE initiative.

The confrontation of knowledge and competence

The EHE initiative was introduced as an attempt to intervene in the relationships between HE teachers, their students and the employers of graduates. In the second half of the 1980s, through this project, the Employment Department saw itself as a catalyst working on behalf of employers who needed enterprising employees. Over 128 higher education institutions in England, Scotland and Wales bid for full or development funding from the Employment Department in the very first round of the initiative, seeking money to introduce enterprise skills into the curriculum (TA, 1989). It seemed that the government had found an interested audience for its ideas of encouraging higher education to produce enterprising graduates. But this high level of institutional response was not always matched by enthusiasm *within* the universities, polytechnics and other institutions.

The initiative was billed as developing enterprising *employees*, who would be able to create and use opportunities, work effectively with others, communicate well and learn throughout their lives. It aimed at breaking down the separation of education and the 'world of work'. Enterprising graduates were meant to know about this world and the real economy. Some of the learning to be enterprising was to take place within real economic settings; and partnership arrangements with employers and assessment involving employers were encouraged. The initiative also had a position on the appropriate relationship of EHE teachers and their students, which was expressed as an endorsement of active styles of learning.

Implicit in all this desire by the Employment Department to impact on HE was, and is, a criticism of the current nature of the 'university'. The Employment Department is concerned with the transformation of students. But is the university also concerned with this? Traditionally, in its own terms, the excellence of the university is measured by the quality of its library (an accumulation of books), the quality of its scholarly outputs (star academicians whose names are celebrated by their fellow academics and whose books represent the reproduction and extension of knowledge accumulated in the libraries), and the number of applicants who are turned away because of the limited number of student places (Stone, 1993). At its worst, this form of life parodies the growth of understanding as a single-minded search by academics for discoveries which are realised in books; it places on a pedestal the pursuit of 'truth', but for the benefit of the privileged few, the students who are not turned away, and who are required to immerse themselves in books.

Despite the power of the pre-modern form, the university can transcend the limitations of 'book fetishism' and, in its effects on students, speak to wider communities of need and power. The reason for this optimism is that the image of the 'university' is something of a stereotype in the sense that it only partially exists. This pre-modern institution is alive and well in the so-called 'old' universities or in parts of the redbricks and the 'new' universities which mimic the old to some extent. But no university (even Oxbridge) is entirely pre-modern. Universities – young and old – are contradictory. They contain pre-modern degree titles and rituals and a good deal of pre-modern teaching and learning. In addition, however, they are clothed in layers of modernism in so far as they teach the metanarratives of philosophy, social theory, literary criticism and science and technology. Modernist ideas exist simultaneously with pre-modern practices. The particularity of this contradiction will vary from one institution to another so that there will be a range of contradictory social relations from Oxford and Cambridge to the new universities. Oxbridge privileges the pre-modern end of the range and the new universities the modernist end. The modernist university stresses employment relevance in its degree offer, together with competencies and transferable skills development in the context of facilitated teaching and learning experiences. This modernist approach is partly resource led in so far as it is a response to the pressures of mass higher education. The mass market drowns the possibility of replicating the Oxbridge tutorial system and pressures the modernist university library to the point where customised teaching packs begin to displace the book. Lack of resources may push the modernist university to adapt its teaching and learning practices but in addition such institutions contain strong believers in modernism who are busily converting their colleagues.

But the universities, over the last ten years, have undergone a profound series of changes. These changes have not been experienced everywhere in every faculty. Some Oxbridge colleges have been minimally affected – most new universities have been transformed. These changes have primarily occurred because of the huge influx of students.

This is not just because of the increase in numbers – which has been considerable – but because the students come from different backgrounds and have different experiences; the traditional form of university has come under attack. Minute by minute, day by day, students' expectations created different relationships and different sets of teaching. When the majority of the students are in their late twenties, do not have A levels but do have children, changes occur.

Within this context, EHE was a small experience of change. But it took place within that wider context of change. The problem with EHE, as experienced by some HE teachers, is the double threat to their status within the educational system. The initiative threatened the supremacy of knowledge by supporting the importance of skills in the curriculum, and it threatened the centrality of the academic role by advocating active learning by students and a partnership role for employers.

The academic role needs clarification if the anxieties are to be fully appreciated. The academic is, traditionally, a researcher and an educator. As a researcher the academic has made discoveries by pointing to new truths (statements or interpretations in a given field) and supplying observations to prove the truth. As an educator, the academic is engaged in transmitting knowledge, which in its highest stage of development is truth.

In practice, the educational role seems to be taking a buffeting given the events of recent years. First, the massive increase in students entering higher education has undermined one of the traditional signs of excellence and has threatened the intellectual claims of academics. 'Around 1.3 million students were enrolled in higher education in 1991/92 . . . 57% up on the 1980/81 total. . . . In 1990/91 338,000 students obtained a higher education qualification (52% up on 1980/81)' (Employment Department, 1994). This in itself undermines the traditional academic: the system now requires the university to accept more people as students, and not turn them away. By traditional standards, the university must be less excellent.

Then there is the fear that efficiency arguments will lead government to force some universities to be just teaching institutions – leaving a small number of universities to have a monopoly of the research funds and activity. The former will cease to be sites of discovery; they will become mere reproducers of knowledge. It is open to question whether the 'intellectual' in the teaching-only university is an intellectual at all:

'It should be noted that 'the intellectual' refers to a social role and not to a total person . . . we normally include teachers and professors among the intellectuals. As a rough approximation, this may be adequate, but it does not follow that every teacher or professor is an intellectual. He may or may not be, depending on the actual nature of his activities. The limiting case occurs when a teacher merely communicates the content of a textbook, without further interpretations or applications. In such cases, the teacher is no more an intellectual than a radio announcer who merely reads a script prepared for him by others. He is then merely a cog in the transmission belt of communicating ideas forged by others' (Merton, 1968).

The pre-modern system of higher education was based on a self-image of academics as society's intellectuals. But only those academics who research and write books were intellectuals in this system. Teachers who merely transmit the content of books were not. Even writers of textbooks who summarise the research and ideas of others are really just part of the transmission belt rather than fully-fledged intellectuals. The separation of universities into teaching- and research-based ones opens the door to the possibility of teachers swamping the researcher-intellectual strata. This is a kind of Braverman-type degradation of academic skills through the scientific management of higher education (Braverman, 1974).

Undoubtedly some HE teachers reacted to the title of the EHE initiative and did not like the idea of developing the personnel for the Thatcher revolution. But the EHE initiative, and other changes such as the development of NVQs, threatens the academic in quite a different (revolutionary) way. The traditional HE system is formed around the notion of the expansion of knowledge through a historical process of advancing and extending knowledge, a progress made possible by the results of research and intellectual work which adds new discoveries and new truth to the existing stock of educational wealth. Knowledge has to be preserved and carried through into new levels of education, but it has also to be expanded by fresh research and intellectual labours. EHE, and NVQs, break with this line of accumulation. They want educational practices which transmit not knowledge but skill (or competence).

Postmodernism

In an argument which is quite distinctive from that offered here, Lyotard has suggested that the university is expected to contribute to the performance (efficiency, for example) of the wider social system. He says:

'universities and the institutions of higher learning are called upon to create skills, and no longer ideals – so many doctors, so many teachers in a given discipline, so many engineers, so many administrators, etc. The transmission of knowledge is no longer designed to train an elite capable of guiding the nation' (Lyotard, 1984).

He clings to seeing this higher learning as the transmission of an organised stock of knowledge, and even develops a vision of computer-ised data banks of knowledge as the culmination of the processes at work. In the UK, the spirit of his remarks also seems to have some relevance. The government is literally demanding (via EHE and NVQs) competence in operational skills and performance skills. Education detects in these demands the statement that society needs people who can do things, not just know things. Education is being challenged using a performance criterion.

Importantly, the EHE initiative revolves around making the student the centre of the learning process (that is, *active* learning) and developing personal skills (such as working with others, communication and so on), while NVQs are based on preparing people who can carry out specific occupational tasks or functions according to high standards of competence. The former challenges HE teachers to relate differently to their 'other' (the student), while the latter challenges them to place a different value on knowledge and performance.

The arrival of the performance criterion in the form of the development of NVQs signalled a crisis in confidence of the educational system's ability to meet the needs of Britain for occupational skills. The educational system was simply not producing skills; it was too busy transmitting knowledge of doubtful relevance and efficacy.

Some, but we stress not all, HE staff found it difficult to respond to this demand for skills. They were committed to, locked into, knowledge as the ultimate academic value. They idealised the learning process as absorbing organised knowledge and they idealised learning by students as learning to appreciate good theory and good evidence in academic books and journals. Learning is defined, accordingly, as purely investment of intellectual energy in taking in information and learning to reflect back the information within formal assessment.

They responded to the demand for skills by withholding, or reluctantly conceding, academic credit for the development and use of such skills by students. Or they universalised their own knowledge-based education practice to the issue of skill development by attempting to discover the truth about the ideological or linguistic codes shaping the demand for skills and their assessment. The question they posed was not how could or should such skills or competences be developed but why should they be developed? Who says so? And for what purposes? This was a critical response aimed at establishing the hegemony of knowledge over skill/ competence. Skill was turned from a curriculum objective, something which students should practice and develop, into a subject for intellectual discussion, something which could become the object of academic knowledge and discourse. Skills (or occupational competencies, eg in selecting staff) became, at least in the minds of some academics, a social construction. They were to be posited as an appearance lacking a material basis. This was the postmodernist response. The criticism made by some academics of the legitimacy of EHE and NVQs ended in the claim that skills or competencies were a social construct. This happened because the traditional academic preoccupation with knowledge had provided a way of placing skill beyond the realm of the real.

The price for this way of coping with the demands for skills/ competencies was to admit extreme subjectivism, which assumed that there is no such thing as skill-in-itself. This radical subjectivism says skill is a label people put on situations. Further back lurked the issue of who was to do this labelling and the acceptability of who this was. The acceptance of this position is the basis of radical perspectivism. Truth is now not absolute but relative. (At least it recognises that others, apart from academics, have a claim on the truth. Unfortunately, it neutralises this gain by insisting that all have the truth, and therefore, nobody does.) We will not respond to this argument in its own terms. We are more concerned to develop a rival position based on a new modernism.

New Modernism

Skill is a property of a person; it is a person's ability to demonstrate a system and sequence of behaviour that are functionally related to attaining a performance goal (Boyatzis, 1982). In contrast, a function (eg selecting staff) is a property of a job; a person uses a set of skills to perform a function effectively. Just to confuse things, while we may equate competences with skills, the NVQ model analyses competences as elements of job functions.

Skill can be applied in any number of situations or contexts. The NVQ framework, which is a competence-based model of assessment of occupational performance, also aims to be valid for a range of situations and specifically requires assessment to check out performance under different ranges of conditions.

Development and assessment of skills (as in the EHE initiative) and functional competences (as in the NVQ model) arguably have different requirements. While a performance of a function in a specified number of situations may be sufficient to testify to an occupational competence, the development and assessment of skill implies a linkage between the situations. The individual who has a skill is encouraged to use that skill by successfully performing in different situations with the skill consisting in the deliberate altering and control of the performance to make it successful. In other words, skill implies the ability to go beyond the present situation. This is well captured in Blauner's remarks on the subject of traditional skill:

'The freedom to determine techniques of work, to choose one's tools, and to vary the sequence of operations, is part of the nature and traditions of craftmanship. Because each job is somewhat different from previous jobs, problems continually arise which require a craftsman to make decisions. Traditional skill thus involves the frequent use of judgement and initiative, aspects of a job which give the worker a feeling of control over his environment' (Blauner, 1964).

This notion of skill fits very comfortably with the EHE initiative (at least as it was officially presented). Enterprising graduates would be able to use their skills (create and use opportunities, work effectively with others, communicate well and learn throughout their lives) in a range of situations irrespective of particular occupational role or functions within that role. These EHE skills are essential for the creation of a work-force which is creative and adaptable. These are the personal qualities which would make it easier for people to acquire, and evolve, the functional competences which occupy centre stage in the NVQ framework. The personal skills of the EHE initiative are metacompetences necessary to the effective exploitation of functional competences.

To obtain the transferable skills of EHE would require a university education which expected students to practise the key skilled behaviours and provided support to do this. As the EHE initiative intended, this would involve student-centred learning activities. It would, moreover, institute a process of learning by discovery through student activity and experimentation. Without the focus in the higher education curriculum on personal skills it is difficult to see how students can have more than a superficial access to knowledge. Academic staff, via their research activities which produce knowledge, experience the legitimation of knowledge; students as passive recipients of transmitted knowledge cannot experience the legitimation of knowledge. A curriculum involving the development of personal skills by students necessitates an active relation to the consumption of knowledge (because it is simultaneously a production of knowledge by the student) and thus secures a more convincing legitimation of the body of knowledge as something which can be used rather than merely acquired.

The postmodernist attack on metanarratives around skills or competences at least recognises the 'multivocality' of higher education, which is more than the NVQ model of competences does. But the fragmentation of the subject in the postmodernist outlook needs to be replaced by a concern for the real subject of education – the student. Likewise, the shift of concern from educational development of knowledge to the development of occupational skills within NVQs needs to reinstate the role of 'discovery', which essentially means the development of *personal* skills by students through student-centred learning activities. The new modernist theme is therefore the all-round development of personal skills which enables people to be active consumers of knowledge and skilful users of occupational competences.

One of the ways in which modernism in the past created a metanarrative about knowledge was to see knowledge as power. This meant that those who gained knowledge were seen as also gaining power. In fact, this did not happen. Knowledge, any knowledge, or more to the point, any knowledge provided at university, did not construct power for those who received it. Some of the things that went along with, say, a degree in early English from Oxbridge, did provide power. Contacts, status, the right way of expressing yourself, all granted power; but knowing the story of Beowulf versus the bog people in Middle English did not.

At the heart of any optimism for modernism is evidence of the potential for new educational practices within the university. This evidence shows that universities can not only emphasise the acquisition of knowledge, they can also emphasise the use of knowledge. Raven (1984) refers to research on Ivy League colleges in the United States which showed that they 'have fostered the willingness and the ability to think critically and to handle cognitive complexity – especially the cognitive complexity involved in understanding social problems'. These colleges develop such competences in their students by exposing them to diverse experiences, creating opportunities for them to practise new styles of behaviour (leadership, innovation, etc), expecting challenging work to be done to high standards, insisting on high standards in independent academic study and providing time for students to explore, reflect and integrate their experiences and understanding. But using knowledge is more than intellectual skills. Part of the responsibility of the new modernism is to demonstrate a relationship between knowledge and skills that provides the individual with power. Knowing how to think in the twenty-first century will be of little use without knowing how to use a wordprocessor and the whole panoply of IT.

New modernism in HE requires a very different teacher/taught relationship and a very different society/university relationship. Universities must open up their resources to the surrounding community and seek to construct a dialectical relationship with it. The university can expand the process of certification to its significant feeder institutions – both educational and non-educational. They can work much more closely with schools and FE colleges to prepare students for degree level courses. Just as importantly, they can work with local employers to expand the certification of employees. This can be achieved by constructing compacts between local employers and universities which are mutually advantageous. Finally, the two can work together to create professional development awards at NVQ level 3 and above. Such relationships – partnerships – break down differences and forge forward-looking and exciting outcomes.

References

Blauner, Robert (1964) *Alienation and Freedom*, University of Chicago Press, p. 43.

Boyatzis, Richard E (1982) *The Competent Manager*, Wiley, Chichester, p. 33.

Braverman, Harry (1974) *Labor and Monopoly Capital*, The Monthly Review, London.

Employment Department (1994), *Labour Market Quarterly Report*, Thay, pp. 12–13.

Lyotard, Jean-Francois (1984) *The Postmodern Condition*, Manchester University Press, p. 48.

Merton, Robert K (1968) *Social Theory and Social Structure*, The Free Press, New York, pp. 263–4.

Raven, John (1984) *Competence in Modern Society*, H K Lewis & Co Ltd, London, p. 140.

Stone, Norman (1993) 'Why we should privatise Oxford University', *The Sunday Times*, 12 December.

Training Agency, Employment Department Group (1989) *Skills Bulletin*, no 8, Spring.

Chapter 4

Supporting Students and Lecturers in the Learning and Teaching of Skills

Adrienne Clarke and Frances Tomlinson

Introduction

In this chapter we describe the development of the teaching of 'skills' on undergraduate programmes in the Business School at the University of North London. We start by discussing the development of skills on BA (Hons) Business Studies (BABS) as this provided the model for skills development in the Business School. This is followed by an account of the 'Business Skills' module on BA (Hons) Accounting and Finance (BAAF). The final sections describe the support given to students through the 'Study Skills and Learning Materials' handbook and the support given to staff through the 'Skills Teaching Handbook'.

The BABS degree programme was launched in 1980. Its main aim was identified as: 'To provide a broad-based and academically rigorous education to honours degree level for those students intending to pursue administrative, managerial and related professional careers' (PNL, 1980). The course was thus defined as having a vocational basis; as being 'for' business as well as 'about' business. Its objectives emphasised the importance of subject disciplines, including mathematics, economics, statistics and behavioural science, as a foundation for business education. Developing the course required lecturers from these different disciplines coming together to produce a coherent programme of study. The disciplines were introduced in the first year; there was no attempt to integrate them at this level.

When the degree was revised in 1984 the aim of providing an academically rigorous, broadbased study of business and its disciplines was retained. However, an additional objective was included, namely: 'To provide an organised interdisciplinary forum for student centred learning which will develop problem solving and communication skills' (PNL, 1984). The structuring of the first two years of the course around disciplines was basically unchanged, but an attempt was made 'to link these disciplines through their respective contributions to business decision making'. The introduction of decision making as a theme represented an attempt to introduce coherence. The vehicle chosen for integration was the 'Business Workshop' introduced into the first and second years of the course. In developing the workshop the course planners drew on their experience of running 'cross modular assignments' on BTEC HND courses when they had been 'impressed by the student motivation, initiative and enthusiasm when undertaking these assignments'.

The Business Workshops were therefore identified as being integrative, as vehicles for skills development, and as 'student centred' in that a considerable amount of the time on the module involved students undertaking project work in small groups, with teaching staff acting as consultants.

The next revision of the degree took place in 1990. The aims were substantially changed, in that although 'academic rigour' was retained less emphasis was placed on subject disciplines. The acquisition and development of transferable skills were specifically included in the course aims, which also referred to the promotion of 'a range of teaching, learning and assessment methods which provide students with the opportunity to develop self-confidence and the ability to work both independently and cooperatively with others' (PNL, 1990). A further departure in terms of defining course aims was represented by the reference to extending 'access to the course to the widest possible group of students who are able to benefit from studying and gaining an award'.

The Business Workshops were retained but their focus was somewhat different from the 1984 version. That syllabus had focused on a number of specific business problems which students would be required to research; skills acquisition was largely a by-product of working with others gathering and presenting data. The 1990 syllabus for the first year workshop identified eight different skills areas, including self-awareness and self-development, study and learning skills, interpersonal skills and problem solving. Diagnosis of students' needs for skills development and the use of experiential exercises were emphasised in describing how students would acquire these skills from the workshop.

Thus over ten years the degree has undergone considerable change; its aims are now much more wide ranging, taking into account the nature and needs of the student population, specifying what skills and competences they should take away from the course and highlighting the importance of the *processes* of teaching, learning and assessment as well as course *content*. The increased significance given to transferable skills can be seen as a response to the more demanding and varied teaching and assessment methods that students now have to cope with, to the wider diversity of the student population (including a significant number of mature entrants without traditional examination-based qualifications) and to the increased difficulties many students were experiencing in obtaining sandwich placements.

The continuing process of change and transformation has not been unproblematic, however, and the area of 'skills teaching' has often been particularly controversial. In the eyes of some lecturers the introduction of skills units threatened the 'academic' integrity of the course in a number of ways. First, it was interpreted as having a 'remedial' aspect, that we were spending time helping students improve in areas such as basic study skills that they should have acquired earlier in their education and which we were not well qualified to teach. Secondly, skills was seen as an 'easy option', undemanding academically with no examination and no formal lectures. Thirdly, because skills were not seen to be based in any particular academic discipline, it was thought anybody could teach them. Several specialist staff were appointed in the Business School specifically to coordinate teaching in this area; however skills units were also staffed by teachers across the discipline areas, some of whom had not used experiential teaching methods before.

These objections were reflected in some students' attitudes towards skills units. Teaching skills to full-time undergraduates is very different from teaching similar programmes on post-experience management courses, where the validity and relevance of these skills to the students is immediately obvious since they continually rely on them. The way in which some of these difficulties have been addressed are dealt with in the following section which examines the Business Skills module on BAAF.

The Business Skills module on BAAF

During the resubmission process for BAAF, which took place during 1988 and 1989, it seemed as though there would be no place for a 'skills' module. The resubmission group stated that the module 'Business Seminars' (the module through which skills were developed, although this was not its sole purpose) had 'to some extent served its purpose and might not be included in any new scheme' (PNL, 1989). The conclusion of the group was that 'these [skills] could now be developed more effectively in other mainstream units, and would be more meaningfully developed in them as opposed to a separate module.' An evaluation exercise carried out with past and current students came to a similar conclusion.

However, other developments were taking place on BABS and several of the BABS skills tutors were involved in the BAAF development team. These developments brought about increased support for the original arguments in favour of a separate module.

The initial programme was drawn up in consultation with members of the course team who were asked to identify the skills they wanted included in the module. The skills identified were very much in line with those identified by the group developing the module. Nevertheless it was felt that the consultation exercise had been a worthwhile way of involving those who harboured doubts about the need for such a module.

The module was based on experiential learning enabling students to practise the skills through a range of activities and exercises. One of the key elements was the opportunity for peer feedback which most of the students found challenging but helpful: 'The peer assessment was a very good idea as knowing what other people recognise in you in terms of your strengths (and weaknesses) can give you more confidence and help you better yourself' (1993/4 evaluation by student group).

With very few exceptions, the students have been positive about the module. Moreover, some of these 'exceptions' did have a change of heart: 'I felt skills was not necessary and that I was wasting time which I could have spent on other subjects. Given a second chance I would put in a lot more effort than I did this time' (1990/91 evaluation by student group).

Although students enjoyed the interactive and participative methods used in the module, they did highlight the difference in style and method between this module and the more 'traditional' methods used in other subjects. Moreover, the difficulties some of them experienced in getting to grips with economics, accounting and quantitative methods in their first year tended to preoccupy their attention so that their learning from the skills module was inevitably perceived as less significant for their survival on the course. In addition, the fact that part of their assessment was based on a group assignment created difficulties for some students; some groups were able to work cooperatively and productively but others were more conflict torn, particularly when some members didn't appear to contribute, 'free-riding' on the efforts of others. Such situations were particularly frustrating for those who felt that the group grade did not reflect their individual abilities.

To resolve the issue of individual versus group assessment greater weight is now given to the individual rather the group. For example, students are now required to produce an individual record outlining the part they played in the group process. This forms part of the assessment which is based on a research project, is continuous and is divided into five phases including peer and self-assessment. The following sums up the general feeling in relation to the assessment process: 'The presentation and essay were good ways of getting involved with other people and working in groups. I find it a bit difficult to assess myself, but I do assess myself honestly' (1994/5 evaluation by student group).

Supporting students – the 'Study Skills and Learning Materials' handbook

The 'Study Skills and Learning Materials' handbook was first issued to all first-year students in September 1988. The handbook covered areas such as reading, taking notes and writing essays which one would expect to find in a study skills book. However, it also included sections on working in groups, report writing and making presentations. The aim of the handbook was to enable students to become 'more effective' in carrying out these tasks.

At the time the handbook was produced the majority of students were not taught skills via a separate module. However, as the number of skills modules has increased the handbook has become their main text, providing an important reference for both students and skills tutors. According to one student the handbook was: 'the course bible and dictionary' (1990/91 evaluation by student group).

The handbook is now in its seventh year. Feedback from students and lecturers has resulted in the inclusion of new sections: 'Dealing with case studies', which reflected the increasing use of the case study both in teaching and assessment, and 'Applying for jobs and going for interviews', which was included at the request of students, reflecting their concerns about life after the Business School.

The handbook has always been favourably received: 'The skills handbook has been very useful and I have referred back to it on numerous occasions' (1993/4 evaluation); 'The skills handbook is extremely important and I think it will stay with me as a reference until the completion of my studies' (1991/2 evaluation).

We now plan to produce an open learning version of the skills handbook. With an increasing number of students entering under-graduate programmes in year two, we need to ensure that these students are not disadvantaged in relation to those students who have taken a skills module in their first year. However, it will be difficult to simulate the frustrations and pleasures that students experience when doing a group project for the first time: 'The presentation was good because it allowed us to work in groups and so we learned from each other and also helped each other' (1993/4 evaluation).

The 'Skills Teaching Handbook'

In developing skills modules we built up a bank of exercises. These derived from a variety of sources; some we developed ourselves, some we found in written texts and the origins of still others were unknown. This experience enabled us to identify what worked and what did not, and to adapt materials to fit the needs of our student population. We were particularly concerned that the materials should reflect the diversity of our student body.

The expansion of skills teaching meant that increased numbers of staff were now involved in teaching skills. Many did not regard themselves as 'skills experts' and had relatively little experience of working in this area. However, on each programme there was usually one more experienced lecturer who acted as module 'coordinator', taking overall responsibility for devising the programme and providing materials for the other tutors.

To facilitate the process of sharing materials and to ease the work of the coordinator it was decided to develop a handbook for skills tutors. We were supported in its production by the university's Enterprise in Higher Education programme. The purpose of the handbook is to share 'good practice' in skills teaching. The introduction gives advice on the *processes* involved; emphasising the facilitation of student learning through providing organised experiential 'events' as opposed to didactic teaching. Suggestions are given for the structuring of sessions, the forming of small groups for student activities and the use of observers. The rest of the handbook is divided into sections, each introducing a specific skills area and containing a number of exercises together with examples of handouts, slides and references to further reading. The instructions for each exercise are fairly detailed, specifying its aims, the context in which it is useful, the time taken and suggestions for discussion points. The handbook is presented in a looseleaf format with the intention of adapting and adding to exercises in the light of our ongoing experience.

The increased pressure on lecturers in higher education provided part of the incentive for producing the handbook; getting teaching teams together is proving more difficult and resources for skills coordinators have been reduced. The processes involved in teaching and learning skills are not always straightforward, students need to get actively involved. This may require them overcoming certain inhibitions and embarrassments and some activities, such as giving and receiving feedback on personal behaviour, are potentially quite exposing. We believe that we should not ask students to undergo processes that we have not been through ourselves; team building and staff development sessions are needed to achieve this. The handbook is not intended to substitute for staff development, but to support it. This has already happened; material from the handbook was used to demonstrate using role play to teach group work skills during a staff development session for lecturers in the Humanities and Teacher Education faculty under the university's EHE programme.

Conclusion

To some extent the teaching of skills to undergraduates is still a controversial issue within the Business School. It is interesting to note that although women are in the minority among the lecturing staff as a whole the majority of staff teaching skills are women (exclusively so on BAAF).

However developments over the last ten years have on the whole encouraged skills teaching. The differences between teaching and assessment methods used for teaching skills and other subjects have tended to diminish; staff across the Business School increasingly use methods such as group project work and assessed oral presentations.

Undergraduate provision throughout the school is currently being incorporated into a modular scheme and a decision has been taken to include a compulsory skills module at preliminary level. Modularisation forms part of an increasingly complex educational environment, exacerbated by the increased numbers of students in seminar groups. More pressure is therefore put on students to become 'independent learners'; many of them have responded by forming study groups (as encouraged in the student handbook).

Finally the requirement that all students have the opportunity of participating in personal competence profiling by 1996 has focused attention even more on the skills acquired by students during their studies and their transferability beyond higher education (see Section 2 of this book). A dedicated skills module at the beginning of their programme provides a starting point, but this has to be supported through the further integration of a skills-based approach to teaching and learning across the curriculum.

References

Polytechnic of North London (PNL) (1980) *BA Business Studies Definitive Course Document 1980*, PNL, London.

PNL (1984) *Business Studies Definitive Course Document 1984*, PNL, London.

PNL (1989) *BA Accounting and Finance Course Review 1989*, PNL, London.

Chapter 5

Student Enterprise:
A Forum for Building on
Transferable Skills

Ruth Watson

Student Enterprise came about largely due to the decision of some Enterprise in Higher Education (EHE) institutions to incorporate student participation on a 'management' rather than a representative level in their EHE initiative. The first institution to adopt this model was Chester College. The rationale for adopting a management structure which included provision for a student manager was that the EHE initiative would reach into the student community by commanding peer respect. It became evident during the initial phase of the EHE initiative, when funding had been targeted mainly at staff and curriculum development, that many students were unaffected and unaware of the concept and practice of EHE. Indeed, there were many misconceptions among students about what 'enterprise' meant and many different, often negative interpretations were placed on the whole EHE ethos.

By far the greatest challenge faced by the new Student Enterprise managers was that of raising awareness of the EHE intiative's aims and objectives among the student community. As more and more EHE institutions adopted the student management model a National Student

Enterprise Network evolved and it became clear that a set of common themes and values was emerging upon which Student Enterprise managers could build. These central themes were adopted in different ways according to the scope and role of the individual Student Enterprise managers' remit and institutional objectives. However, the core activities that were to be encouraged and developed throughout the EHE institutions became known collectively as 'Student Enterprise'. Student Enterprise has greatly assisted in creating mechanisms by which students' understanding, awareness and perception of EHE can be developed hand in hand with staff and curriculum projects.

Delegates at the first national Student Enterprise conference, held at Chester College of Higher Education in January 1991, discussed the rationale and objectives of the Enterprise in Higher Education initiative, and looked closely at its aims, which were to help students become effective lifelong learners with a knowledge of working life, to develop transferable skills, to change the way in which people are educated by bringing education into society through a three-way partnership between institutions, students and employers and to enhance student self-confidence.

On debating what opportunities enterprise should afford students, development and training in interpersonal and transferable skills and providing experience of skills beyond the academic world were given high priority. These aims could be achieved through providing students with the resources and information needed in order to participate more actively in their own learning experience, and by providing opportunities for students to participate in additional extra-curricular activities and training to enhance skills development. While much of the former had begun to be addressed by staff and curriculum developments, the latter had largely been neglected in terms of the EHE initiative. Of course it is true that students' unions have always provided for student development indirectly, not only by providing the opportunity for students to become sabbatical officers and to run clubs and societies, but by providing training for them to do so successfully. However, the enterprise approach was to provide an opportunity for students to become aware of the *skills* they were developing throughout their time in higher education, both at an academic and extra-curricular level, and of how to record and later give evidence of those skills which would be invaluable to them, not only in the career pathway of their choice but for their own personal development and participation in society.

Regional Student Enterprise networks

Student Enterprise practitioners (managers, officers, coordinators, students' union officers and any students who share an interest and enthusiasm for Student Enterprise) have continued to network at national and regional levels since the first conference in 1991, where the importance of networks to facilitate useful exchange of information and good practice has been identified. The creation of regional networks was therefore a logical progression. Regional Student Enterprise networks have been operating in the North, the South and the Midlands. These networks have played a major role in raising awareness of the EHE initiative and the potential for personal and skills development among the nation's student communities. The regional networks have been able to do this by providing a forum in which Student Enterprise practitioners can come together and share experiences, ideas and models of good practice. These networks also provide training and support for their members, who often find themselves in a unique and therefore isolated position at their institution.

The support, encouragement and expertise the network provides assists the Student Enterprise manager in the initiation, set-up and administration of schemes and projects. These projects help to develop skills in students. Regional and national Student Enterprise networks are constantly looking for ways to embed schemes and projects of this nature at their institutions, and for ways to continue the innovation and ideas that Student Enterprise and the EHE ethos encompass. To this end the most recent national Student Enterprise conference, hosted by the Student Enterprise managers of Portsmouth and Manchester Universities at Stoke Rochford Hall in January 1995, had as its theme 'Developing Potentials' and was well attended by Student Enterprise managers, EHE directors, students' union sabbaticals, the National Union of Students (NUS), and members of the Employment Department. The burning issue was how to ensure the continuation of student development which encourages the growth of personal transferable skills through student-centred learning and extra-curricular activity after EHE funding runs out.

Student development and transferable skills

The areas of student development referred to at the Developing Potentials conference covered a range of schemes, activities and projects that involve student participation, leadership and innovation. Many of these activities, such as participation in clubs, societies and student-led projects, had been in place long before the EHE initiative came along, and are a credit to the vision of their particular institutions and students' unions. However, many are schemes which have been actively taken up by Student Enterprise in order to provide students with an added opportunity for developing their potential, outside of this conventional student experience, and in particular to provide skills training for students who, for whatever reason, would not go down the traditional route of belonging to clubs and societies.

This is all the more necessary given the increasingly diverse nature of the student body, which nowadays consists of many more mature students, access students and students with disabilities. For many of these students, university or college is in the same town or city in which they live, and they may have differing needs and commitments from that of the traditional A level entrant who studies away from home, free from external or family commitments. In order to provide an opportunity for *all* students to become familiar with the concept and ethos of transferable skills, Student Enterprise has taken up certain projects which may appeal to both traditional and non-traditional students.

Extra-curricular schemes and projects

Popular projects that are recognised as a useful vehicle for developing a student's potential, confidence and valuable personal transferable skills include volunteer work, mentoring and tutoring schemes. Student Enterprise managers have taken on the set-up and administration or coordination of these schemes and, more importantly, they have succeeded in embedding them within their institution so that they have become a permanent option for their students. These schemes, such as the Student Tutoring scheme, which recruits students to assist teachers in local schools, all provide an opportunity for students to develop existing and gain new skills.

The Student Tutoring scheme is part of an initiative called 'Aiming for a College Education', which is sponsored by BP. This programme was developed in order to provide school pupils with a role model (the student) who could stimulate in them an interest in continuing their education on leaving school. This is done by providing primary and secondary schools and sixth form colleges with students who assist the teacher in the classroom. The students usually work with pupils either individually or in small groups, and through their contribution are able to make classes more interesting and stimulating. The areas in which the students can help in class is varied. Either they can assist with a subject-specific class related to their own studies, such as maths, science, English, history, art and languages, or they can help out generally. For example students may be asked to give individual help to children with reading and writing, or to interpret for children for whom English is not their first language or to help with children who have special or different needs. Students can also help out with drama, music and dance and physical education.

Students who participate in the scheme are as
selves to help at a school for half a day per week o
after which they receive a certificate for their
Enterprise manager recruits students for the schei
with some basic training before finding them
Students completing the Student Tutoring schen
munication and problem-solving skills, as well as
that comes from reinforcing their academic su
different level. Likewise students who volunteer fc
given the opportunity to develop new practical
practice their existing academic and vocational sk
schemes of this sort around (such as Student Con
organise student volunteers to work in all secto
Students who participate in these projects, while
service to society, also gain work experience at
could be cutting grass, decorating, setting up
pensioners on an outing. Whatever they do, they
and have the chance to develop a variety of skill!

The training of student representatives, whicl
carried out successfully either by students' union
now has the additional support of the Student En
can put another view forward which highlights
student is gaining by performing this importar
Enterprise managers have extended the scope of
training to include more specific workshops on e
communication skills for use at higher meeting
employers are being asked to participate in the i
For example, at the University of Aberdeen, Shell l
for student representatives on 'Committee and
Training student representatives in these other ar
support and effective use of students in this impc
their own personal development.

Student job centres

Many Student Enterprise managers have been in
the establishment of student job centres, run
institution. This idea is becoming increasingly
successful implementation of student job cen
Metropolitan and Coventry Universities. Not
student hardship by helping students to find par
with their studies, but they provide an ideal tra
experience and skills development.

Personal transferable skills

Student Enterprise encourages student ow
activities and positively encourages student-le
isation of events. Many institutions have
committees or teams set up by Student
consultation on all aspects of student develop
become so successful that the students runnin
independently. For example, the Student Liaisc
of Portsmouth now invites the Student Enterp
meetings, which are arranged and carried o
selves.

Student Enterprise provides a forum in
transferable skills can be addressed. The
Enterprise often call for hard work and extra e
fun and enjoyable. For example, every year a
teams made up of students, academics and emp
annual 'Luton Challenge', which involves e
mastermind-type quizzes, comic sketches, ly
and outdoor survival activities – all in fancy dr
and hugely enjoyable way to develop one's
skills.

Once students are involved in such activ
interested in other means of increasing their po
is working for the continuation of student
Student Enterprise committees, teams and net
Student Enterprise managers can continue to
ideas and innovations for building on the con

student experience, and in particular to provide skills training for students who, for whatever reason, would not go down the traditional route of belonging to clubs and societies.

This is all the more necessary given the increasingly diverse nature of the student body, which nowadays consists of many more mature students, access students and students with disabilities. For many of these students, university or college is in the same town or city in which they live, and they may have differing needs and commitments from that of the traditional A level entrant who studies away from home, free from external or family commitments. In order to provide an opportunity for *all* students to become familiar with the concept and ethos of transferable skills, Student Enterprise has taken up certain projects which may appeal to both traditional and non-traditional students.

Extra-curricular schemes and projects

Popular projects that are recognised as a useful vehicle for developing a student's potential, confidence and valuable personal transferable skills include volunteer work, mentoring and tutoring schemes. Student Enterprise managers have taken on the set-up and administration or coordination of these schemes and, more importantly, they have succeeded in embedding them within their institution so that they have become a permanent option for their students. These schemes, such as the Student Tutoring scheme, which recruits students to assist teachers in local schools, all provide an opportunity for students to develop existing and gain new skills.

The Student Tutoring scheme is part of an initiative called 'Aiming for a College Education', which is sponsored by BP. This programme was developed in order to provide school pupils with a role model (the student) who could stimulate in them an interest in continuing their education on leaving school. This is done by providing primary and secondary schools and sixth form colleges with students who assist the teacher in the classroom. The students usually work with pupils either individually or in small groups, and through their contribution are able to make classes more interesting and stimulating. The areas in which the students can help in class is varied. Either they can assist with a subject-specific class related to their own studies, such as maths, science, English, history, art and languages, or they can help out generally. For example students may be asked to give individual help to children with reading and writing, or to interpret for children for whom English is not their first language or to help with children who have special or different needs. Students can also help out with drama, music and dance and physical education.

Students who participate in the scheme are asked to commit themselves to help at a school for half a day per week over a ten-week period, after which they receive a certificate for their effort. The Student Enterprise manager recruits students for the scheme and provides them with some basic training before finding them a suitable placement. Students completing the Student Tutoring scheme gain valuable communication and problem-solving skills, as well as gaining the confidence that comes from reinforcing their academic subject knowledge at a different level. Likewise students who volunteer for community work are given the opportunity to develop new practical skills or to put into practice their existing academic and vocational skills. There are various schemes of this sort around (such as Student Community Action) which organise student volunteers to work in all sectors of the community. Students who participate in these projects, while providing a valuable service to society, also gain work experience at a different level. They could be cutting grass, decorating, setting up a database or taking pensioners on an outing. Whatever they do, they enjoy new experiences and have the chance to develop a variety of skills.

The training of student representatives, which has previously been carried out successfully either by students' unions or academic registry, now has the additional support of the Student Enterprise manager, who can put another view forward which highlights the new skills that a student is gaining by performing this important role. Many Student Enterprise managers have extended the scope of student representative training to include more specific workshops on effective committee and communication skills for use at higher meeting level. More recently, employers are being asked to participate in the running of workshops. For example, at the University of Aberdeen, Shell UK provide a workshop for student representatives on 'Committee and communication skills'. Training student representatives in these other areas is important in the support and effective use of students in this important role, and also for their own personal development.

Student job centres

Many Student Enterprise managers have been involved at some level in the establishment of student job centres, run by students, at their institution. This idea is becoming increasingly popular following the successful implementation of student job centres at Cardiff, Leeds Metropolitan and Coventry Universities. Not only do they address student hardship by helping students to find part-time work that fits in with their studies, but they provide an ideal training ground for work experience and skills development.

Student job centres are run in a variety of ways. In some instances, such as at Coventry, students are accredited for the work they do, and in others they are paid. Whatever method is used, the students who help run the centres are all gaining valuable skills and work experience. Job shops provide students with information on suitable local job opportunities, vacation work and casual vacancies within the university and students' union. In addition, the job shop also provides students with information on personal skills development workshops and seminars available to them.

Student job shops provide students with the opportunity to gain new and develop existing personal transferable skills, whether they participate in the running of them, or are patrons. Student Enterprise managers have played an important role in helping set up student job centres and by focusing on and highlighting the opportunity they provide for skills development.

Student induction

The EHE initiative places much emphasis on the need to develop students' transferable skills and to encourage student-centred learning. In pursuit of this aim many projects have been undertaken to develop the curriculum in such a way that it reflects capability-based and employment-related aspects of learning. However, while a lot of effort and resources have gone into staff and project development, there is still a need to persuade *students* of the benefits of these changes.

The drive to raise student awareness has always been one of the most important elements of the Student Enterprise initiative, and it is in this area that a very important channel of communication has been opened up. This task has been undertaken in various ways, the most effective being the use of student induction weeks, freshers and information fairs. At these events Student Enterprise managers have an ideal opportunity to give presentations to students about both Student Enterprise activities and the benefits of personal and skills development.

It is important that students become aware of why they are being asked to conduct their studies in sometimes new and innovative ways. For example at the University of North London, where a system of student profiling is being introduced, it is essential that students are fully aware of what profiling means and how it will benefit them, if it is to be carried out successfully. Most Student Enterprise managers are recent graduates or students on a sabbatical and therefore provide a credible role model for the students they are addressing. It is this grassroots approach of trying to get students switched on to the idea of transferable skills that often works best.

Personal transferable skills

Student Enterprise encourages student ownership of its ideas and activities and positively encourages student-led participation and organisation of events. Many institutions have student liaison groups, committees or teams set up by Student Enterprise managers for consultation on all aspects of student development. In fact, many have become so successful that the students running them now operate quite independently. For example, the Student Liaison Group at the University of Portsmouth now invites the Student Enterprise manager along to its meetings, which are arranged and carried out by the students themselves.

Student Enterprise provides a forum in which the concepts of transferable skills can be addressed. The projects run by Student Enterprise often call for hard work and extra effort, but they are always fun and enjoyable. For example, every year at the University of Luton, teams made up of students, academics and employers get together for the annual 'Luton Challenge', which involves each team in a variety of mastermind-type quizzes, comic sketches, lyrical composition, games and outdoor survival activities – all in fancy dress. This is an imaginative and hugely enjoyable way to develop one's teamwork and leadership skills.

Once students are involved in such activities they soon become interested in other means of increasing their potential. Student Enterprise is working for the continuation of student development. Through Student Enterprise committees, teams and networks, both students and Student Enterprise managers can continue to come together to discuss ideas and innovations for building on the concept of transferable skills.

Section Two:

Profiling and Transferable Skills

The process of profiling encourages students to become aware of the skills, abilities and qualities they possess or may want to develop. The process can help student learning by providing learning goals, by articulating what constitutes evidence for the attainment of these goals, and by relating assessment tasks to learning targets. It can also facilitate preparation for employment. In the latter domain, profiling may be invaluable in the process of preparing a CV, or it may help a student prepare for a job interview. Indeed, the process of encouraging students to think about the potentially transferable skills they may be gaining can be useful preparation for the workplace itself.

The Academic Board of the University of North London has adopted a policy making the profiling of personal competence an entitlement for all students. The following is the definition of profiling agreed by the Board: 'a process which enables students to articulate and, where appropriate, act upon, what they have learned, to review and reflect upon this learning and to record their achievements and communicate these to others'. The Board then agreed an implementation strategy which will make profiling available to all students by 1996.

The Academic Board adopted this policy, following three years of piloting of a range of types of profiling system, and following extensive consultation involving many staff and students at the university, as well as employers with whom people at the university have connections. The

university deliberately took the view that approaches to profiling should be owned by school or faculty teams, and so it did not develop centrally a 'model' profiling system. This has had the advantage that profiling systems have been developed that are relevant to particular subject areas, but it has the potential disadvantage that an individual student on the university's modular scheme may encounter different approaches to the process. The university has also strongly emphasised, both in the definition adopted by Academic Board, and in the extensive staff development programme that has been taking place, that it is the process of profiling that is important – in other words, the process of developing, on the one hand, a person's awareness of the skills or abilities they may possess, and, on the other, a recognition of the skills or abilities that they would like to develop. Many of the employers who have been consulted have emphasised this; that it is not the production of voluminous documentation that matters. The documentation is likely to be valuable more as an aid in the process of profiling than it is as a validated means of certification of skills that are 'objectively' present. The process itself, moreover, will not work unless students are helped to find opportunities for gaining skills they may decide they would like to acquire.

Evaluations of the pilots have produced mixed results: some of these results are described in the chapters that follow. On the positive side, in the BABS programme, and the year abroad, for example, students and employers argued that the process of profiling provided a framework for learning that was previously absent.

In other areas, evaluations have revealed that some students have failed to respond to the invitation to think about their skills development, while others have expressed very strong support both for the principles behind the profiling process and for the process itself. Staff teams at the university are learning from the experience of one another and from experience elsewhere.

The chapters in this section of the book describe some of the profiling systems that have been developed in the university and articulate some of the ways in which these systems help facilitate the development of transferable skills.

The chapter by Sue Bailey describes profiling in Consumer Studies; that by Paul Joyce et al. outlines a profiling system developed for the placement year in the BA Business Studies degree. Dave Taylor provides a picture of the process of development of a profiling system for students on Social Science degree programmes and Ken MacKinnon outlines the profiling system developed for students of Film Studies. Inge Weber-Newth and Martha Dueñas-Tancred describe a profiling system developed to provide a means of accreditation for the concurrent learning acquired by language students on their year abroad. Finally Barbara Page and Anne Brockbank, respectively from chemistry and Business Studies, provide two further perspectives.

Overall the chapters describe a range of profiling systems, designed to fulfil a number of purposes. The overriding aim in each case, however, remains that of providing a framework that is designed to help students to develop their transferable skills.

Chapter 6

Profiling Work Experience in Consumer Studies

Sue Bailey

The market for consumer products and services has grown dramatically over the last 15 years. This growth is unlikely to slow down. However, the increasing sophistication of products and awareness by consumers of issues related to food, materials and services that affect their daily lives has put emphasis on the need for trained specialists.

Since the mid-1980s there has been a shift towards courses with Consumer Studies or Science in their titles and away from Home Economics titled courses. This reflects the wider employment opportunities that have developed, as well as substantial evolution in both areas. The recent strengthening of the status of Food within Technology in the National Curriculum and the recognition of high quality teaching in the Home Economics area by the Department for Education (DFE) indicates the support for the subject area.

There are currently over 20 degree courses in the Consumer Studies area. Nationally, from its inception until recently, in Consumer Studies and related areas 500–600 students graduate annually (CNAA, 1992). Employer demand remains healthy for these graduates who possess knowledge and skills that employers want.

Consumer Studies specialists, for example Home Economists, aim to provide scientific and technical skills relating to the creation, marketing,

57

retailing, management and use of consumer products and services; they are involved in the development of products and services that match consumer needs. Courses such as the BSc (Hons) Food and Consumer Studies degree and BTEC HND in Consumer Studies at the University of North London seek to develop the knowledge-base and provide a means for development of these skills.

Short work placements

Historically, Consumer Studies and similar allied courses have had short work experience placements as an integral part of degree and diploma courses. Two of the major aims of such placements have been to give students an insight into the working environment and to develop interpersonal skills alongside work-based skills and knowledge. An extensive research study of such placements concluded that 'there should be an attempt to effectively communicate the objectives of the placement to the placement agencies' (Cross, 1988, p.17, section 3.3). This was perceived both in terms of overall objectives and student-specific objectives.

This chapter will discuss the development of monitoring transferable skills with current University of North London Consumer Studies degree students, through the mechanism of short work placements. The main focus of the chapter is a description of the EHE project that considered the most efficient method of recording of skills development and setting of objectives and resulted in the creation and implementation of student and employer placement booklets.

At a conference following up the CNAA research (see Cross, 1988) it was suggested that placement supervisors should be involved in setting up student-specific objectives. This was subsequently included in the Code of Practice for Short Work Experience Placements (Bath, 1989). This highlighted the value of involving students in negotiating placement objectives as criteria for assessing their progress. Since the publication of the Code, many academic institutions have modified their approach to placements, hence the need for re-evaluating the process and intention.

Developing the profiling project

A clear mechanism for gaining the most efficient use of the short time students are out on placement and focusing on the development of skills and recording skills development was perceived to be necessary; this formed the basis of the project proposal. The project was funded through an EHE grant as part of the university's commitment to developing student competences, their assessment and assimilation into learning.

The aim of the project therefore was to develop a suitable skills profiling system and improve the use of the work experience period for

BSc Food and Consumer Studies students. The project was also aimed to ensure that employers recognised the importance of individual skills development as a major focus of the work placement, rather than, as occasionally happens, just 'giving them a job to do'. A smaller comparative study was also carried out on the suitability of a modified skills profiling system with first-year BTEC HND Consumer Studies students. This is described briefly towards the end of this chapter as the main focus was on the degree module.

The most suitable type of profiling system was thought to be a formative profiling system. This is a combination of forms described in 'Profiling in Higher Education' as a 'negotiated outcomes' profile (Fenwick et al., 1992, p.11) together with a personal development profile. To achieve this involved creating a method of recording the level of possession of skills relevant to the subject area and ensuring students and employers jointly discussed and set achievable objectives.

Objectives set for the project were to:

- develop a profiling format to encompass the pre- and post-placement achievement of learning objectives;
- tighten up the methodology of assessment;
- develop a learning contract negotiated between student, industrial and academic tutors;
- develop company/organisational profiles as placement briefings for new placement students.

The work placement module

Food and Consumer Studies students have the option of taking the work placement module as a third-year unit of the BSc Modular Science degree scheme. This is based on a 4–6-week unpaid placement typically in the summer vacation before the third year. There is also the option of one day a week during the first semester of the third year. The assessment for this unit consists of two reports and a viva.

The main aims of the module are to apply and adapt the principles studied in an academic environment to the workplace and to provide the basics for further study in the third year. The objectives therefore can be summarised as gaining working environment experience, relating academic study to practice, developing personal and interpersonal skills, awareness of departmental structure and culture, career choice preparation, technical development and final-year project ideas.

The work placement module is one that any student – such as a biochemist or ecologist from the School of Life Sciences – can choose. To ensure a level of comparability between different subject areas and to allow for credit for development of skills the report format was changed in 1994 from a single project style report to two reports. The first report now includes an analysis of the placement and the student's skills acquisition and the second report is based on an academic area, relating it to learning developed in the workplace. Students keep a log-book detailing their skills development which is used as a basis for the first placement report. Students also have a viva.

The Food and Consumer Studies students form the greatest number of students taking this degree module so the project considered the development of a skills profiling system solely with them.

Group feedback strategy was used as a technique to canvass the students' opinions of the strengths and weaknesses of the module and its operation. Although the technique is limited in terms of its reliability and application to a range of different areas within an institution, it is a highly practical, low-cost, high response rate technique involving a high level of student participation, including debate and agreement on collective suggestions. Meetings were held with students – first with third-year students who had undertaken placements the previous summer, then with second-year students planning for placement. These meetings were structured so small groups of students could express their opinions through discussion. Opinions were summarised and comments from each group presented to the whole group and a consensus reached.

After evaluation of comments from third-year students who had taken an earlier version of the module, it was felt that, although students were obviously aware of the benefits of the work placement module and were very positive about its value, their perceptions of it for personal skills development was limited. Concerns voiced by students included limited employer expectations and the quality of the placement varying depending on the organisation. Many students suggested that the work placement module should be compulsory.

Students perceptions of valuable skills

To gain a measure of skills that students perceived to be valuable, second-year students were consulted. Students discussed in small, focused groups which were the important skills they thought that placements should develop. These were then summarised and presented to the whole group for discussion and prioritising. Skills areas were summarised as:

- communication;
- intellectual – including research, problem solving, organisation and planning;
- technical skills – creative, aesthetic, work related;
- interpersonal – integration with others, team work, time management, responsibility, discipline, self-confidence, appreciation of other cultures, problem solving;

- numerical – report production, results presentation.

Noticeable omissions were that there was no separation of communication skills into areas such as formal and informal means of communication or spoken and written forms, nor any consideration of specialist techniques such as presentations, reports or articles. Interpersonal skills did not include 'negotiating' or the ability to identify a target and reach it. Numerical skills were limited since 'information technology' and 'using and interpreting data' were both specifically excluded.

After compilation of this summary the project team spent time considering the range of different ways other projects had divided skills categories. The object was to combine features of current students' suggestions with skills suggestions from other sources and relate these to previously identified subject-specific skills. These transferable skills had previously been identified by students as suitable for acquisition on a Food and Consumer Studies degree course (Kitson, 1992). The synthesis of skills identified of primary importance would then be used for the skills development form. This would be tested as a draft with students and employers.

Developing placement booklets

Suitable documentation was then developed to make explicit the responsibilities of students and employers. To create a concise, usable format, two A5 sized booklets (one for students and one for employers) were chosen, as they would be compact and relatively cheap to reproduce. There would be a centrally detachable learning contract form in the student version, with a reduced sample of this in the employers' booklet. This replaced the range of documentation previously provided. Ideas for the creation and use of learning contracts were usefully clarified in *Contract Learning in Sandwich Placement*, which defines a learning contract as:

'A formal agreement between Learner, Assessor and Mentor about what will be learned, how that learning will be assessed, and the means of achieving that learning.' (Marshall, 1993, p.7)

Both booklets covered aims and objectives of the work placement module, and administration and organisation. Additional elements that the student booklet covered were: guidelines for students on work placements; assessment criteria and guidance for submission; student guidelines for work placement profiling; skills profiling – considering level of ability; skills development targets; individual learning objectives specific to the placement; and the learning contract.

Additional areas covered by the employers booklet were: outline of the course and its structure; expectations of students on work placements;

summary of assessment criteria; guidelines for employers; and guidelines for work placement profiling with samples of student work skills profiling sheets, skills development sheets and the learning agreement.

Discussions with industrialists

Industry representatives were invited to a placement discussion group to consider draft versions of the students' and employers' booklets and to discuss issues of student profiling in the workplace. Representative employers from senior or management level in the food retailing sector, public relations, broadcast media, consumer research, magazine journalism and food manufacture attended.

The discussion group considered issues of matching student and employer objectives, development of students' transferable skills and the structure, monitoring and supervision of short professional placements. The idea of a concise booklet was welcomed. Suggestions for improvement of the employers' booklet were the inclusion of more explicit details about options within the course structure and expectations of students on work placements. The skills profiling was thought to be very suitable with the addition of an environmental/international element. The final skills profile form is as shown in Figure 6.1.

The use of the terminology 'learning contract' was felt to be problematic – 'learning agreement' was considered more suitable by all the employers present, due to the legal overtones of the term 'contract'.

Student responses

Second-year students were presented with draft copies of their student booklet and asked to complete the skills profile sheets after they had undertaken an initial skills exploration exercise. They were also asked to comment on the content, highlighting any areas lacking clarity or giving insufficient information. The students requested assessment details be made as explicit as possible and wanted details of exactly how to set objectives and agree the learning contract with the employer.

Once the modifications had been made to the layout and content of both booklets, students received the final copies. Learning agreements giving dates for assessment submissions were signed by students and the industrial placement tutor, with students retaining a copy.

Trialling the profiling system

Before placement, with tutorial guidance, students completed the skills profile sheets in their booklets, clarifying their skills development proposals and what workplace-specific objectives they intended to develop. Then in their pre-placement interview or in the first week of starting placement students discussed the skills they wished to develop and the workplace-specific objectives to check that these were achievable and how they could be measured. The students also agreed a regular meetings structure with their supervisor for monitoring. Student and supervisor signed the learning agreement and a copy was sent to the workplace tutor for confirmation.

Placement visits were undertaken and comments sought as to the value of the booklets and learning agreement. Positive responses were given, such as:

Employer: It helped to focus ideas for the student and employer. . . . It acted as a good document for assessing how the student was progressing and changing things where necessary.

Student: Made me think in detail what I wanted. I realised that there was a skill I had targeted to develop – computing – during placement that I hadn't had a chance to develop yet.

After the placement students completed their reports and filled in a questionnaire as to the value of the process.

Student feedback

Students were asked whether they felt the objectives of the workplace unit had been achieved. All students felt that the majority of the objectives had been fully achieved, with the exception of usefulness of the placement for project planning. Some students also found that the opportunities for technical development were limited. However, as far as meeting the objective of developing personal and interpersonal skills is concerned 91 per cent of the students agreed that this objective had been fully met and 9 per cent that it had been partially met.

Comments from students included:

'The placement organisation was very supportive and very ready to receive me.'

'Very well organised. We discussed and set the three objectives together using the booklet and skills sheet because it was very easy to see what I would be able to do.'

All students found the skills profile targeting useful or very useful – one commenting that 'it was easy to see at a glance where you improved'. And all found the objectives setting similarly helpful: 'You always know where you stand and what you've done'.

The completion of the work placement module was to hand in the reports and undertake a viva. As part of the marks for the report assessment a poster and a briefing leaflet summarising the benefits of the workplace experience, the work of the department and a typical job profile were completed. The posters and leaflets were then presented as an attended display to second-year students contemplating taking the module.

Employers involved in supervising current students were invited to the poster presentation in order to seek their views on the value of work placement profiling for their particular organisation and to gain a view of other students' work. Employers were very happy with the system and no significant changes were suggested.

Current practice

As the briefing process with the summer 1994 group of students was developmental, the following structure that integrates successful features of this project is now being implemented.

After initial briefing on the general aims and objectives of the work placement module and an introduction to the range of work areas, individual short tutorials are held with students for the discussion of their CV and their career aspirations. Workplace categories and suggested contacts are on the computer-based workplace database system, developed by the author. Students access employer contact entries giving organisational profile details and follow them up, with control being kept over contacts made.

Students then attend a workshop to assess their level of personal development over a range of different skills and to consider the evidence necessary to determine their level of ability. A self-analysis sheet is completed to prompt students' self-awareness before they complete any documentation.

Students are then given the work placement booklets and are expected to complete a categorised double-page section (as shown in Figure 6.1) listing communication skills, problem solving skills, team-work skills, management skills and self-development/personal attributes. Students next have to determine their priorities in terms of skills development in each category as necessary. Placements are contacted, copies of the employers' booklet sent and final arrangements made. The skills and objectives documentation is then used as a focus for discussion with the placement supervisor and the learning agreement is signed and copied to the university tutor.

Students and supervisors have regular meetings to monitor skills developments and achievement of objectives, given time and work constraints. After the placement a second profiling sheet is completed with comments on specific skills developed and clarifying the evidence for achievement that has been presented.

In the autumn term student reports, posters and leaflets are submitted. The first report concentrates on an analysis of the organisation, evidence for personal skills developed and the achievement of personal learning objectives set. The second report is an academic analysis of a specified issue or topic related to the workplace, such as quality assurance in the workplace or matching consumer needs to provision. Vivas are undertaken in the spring term. Final evaluation of the project is awaited as vivas are being assessed at the time of writing.

The system of recognising and tracking the importance of skills development, with some modifications, has also been used with BTEC HND Consumer Studies students. These students seem to be rather less skilled at self-evaluation, which points to the need for student training in skills assessment. As part of the overall university profiling programme, students will increasingly gain expertise in self-evaluation.

The purpose of the profiling approach to the work placement module is to utilise the short placement as efficiently as possible. To summarise the achievement of the objectives of the project – staff and students now feel that students are much more focused and better prepared for their time on placement. This has been borne out by employer comments. It is hoped that this approach can be modified for use with other courses with short workplace-based experience.

Employers benefit from students who are well motivated and have clarified their priorities. Students benefit from being able to bridge both theory and practice and have the satisfaction of developing their skills, achieving their objectives and being able to provide a valued contribution to the organisation.

References

Bath College of Higher Education, (1989) *Code of Practice for Short Work Experience Placements*, Placement Experience Working Party, Bath.

Council for National Academic Awards (CNAA) (1992) *Review of Consumer Studies and Home Economics Degree Courses*, Committee for Consumer and Leisure Studies, CNAA, London.

Cross, C (1988) *Experiential and Vocational Education in Home Economics Courses*, CNAA, Bath.

Fenwick, A, Assiter, A and Nixon, N (1992) *Profiling in Higher Education: Guidelines for the development and use of profiling schemes*, CNAA, London.

Kitson, M (1992) University of North London, unpublished EHE project report.

Marshall, I (1993) *Contract Learning in Sandwich Placement*, Napier University/Employment Department.

Sample of Student Document

Work Skills Profiling – Pre-Placement

Complete this sheet using the following categories
1 Definite ability **2** Some ability **3** Undeveloped ability **4** No experience

COMMUNICATION SKILLS

Ability to express self clearly and well in the following areas:

		1	2	3	4
Writing	Technical report	1	2	3	4
	Project report	1	2	3	4
	Product evaluation report	1	2	3	4
	Feature article	1	2	3	4
Verbal	Ability to speak to a range of people				
	- informally	1	2	3	4
	- formally	1	2	3	4
	- presentation of a case/project	1	2	3	4
Visual	Use of presentation material	1	2	3	4
	Use/awareness of design techniques	1	2	3	4
Numeracy		1	2	3	4

PROBLEM SOLVING SKILLS

	1	2	3	4
Generation of new ideas/ redesign existing ideas/products	1	2	3	4
Research/data collection	1	2	3	4
Task organisation & planning	1	2	3	4
Understand & summarise information	1	2	3	4
Ability to work on own initiative	1	2	3	4

TEAM WORK SKILLS

	1	2	3	4
Working within a group/team	1	2	3	4
Ability to speak clearly and concisely	1	2	3	4
Negotiation	1	2	3	4
Encourage and motivate others	1	2	3	4

COMPUTING SKILLS

Level of keyboard competence	1	2	3	4
Word processing	1	2	3	4
Desk top publishing	1	2	3	4
Statistical data	1	2	3	4
Production of graphics	1	2	3	4
Database management	1	2	3	4
Use of spreadsheets	1	2	3	4

List programmes you have used...

....

....

MANAGEMENT SKILLS

Setting/meeting objectives	1	2	3	4
Leadership ability	1	2	3	4
Resource management	1	2	3	4
Time management	1	2	3	4

SELF DEVELOPMENT/PERSONAL ATTRIBUTES

Personal goal setting	1	2	3	4
Ability to work under pressure	1	2	3	4
Creative talents	1	2	3	4
Self discipline	1	2	3	4
Self confidence	1	2	3	4
International outlook	1	2	3	4
Appreciation of environmental issues	1	2	3	4

Students use this sheet to evaluate their level of skills prior to their placement.

This is then used to complete the skills development sheet and the learning agreement. Students complete these prior to starting the placement, if possible discussing areas at a pre-placement interview. Once feasible objectives and skills development areas have been discussed between placement supervisor and student, the learning agreement can be signed. Students are made aware that time and organisational constraints may mean that not all skills or objectives targeted can be realistically achieved. Ideally the learning agreement would be signed by the end of the first week of placement.

At the end of the placement, students complete another work skills profiling sheet to monitor change.

Comments on how learning objectives were fulfilled and skills developed form part of students placement reports.

Guide for Employers   *Susan Bailey and Ann Page-Wood*

Figure 6.1   *Skills profile form.*

Chapter 7

The Use and Value of Profiling on a BA Business Studies Placement

Stuart Allan, George Blount, Tim Dodd, Sue Johnstone, Paul Joyce, Val Walcott and Nick Winstanley

Introduction

Business Studies degrees in England have long been designed on the sandwich model with a one-year placement in employment inserted between the second and final years of the programme. In many places, and for a long time, there has been a tendency for this to provide a student with experience in which the work-based placement *interrupts* academic, classroom-based learning. Students have found very little of use in their classroom-based studies when they are out on placement, and relatively little use has been made of the placement experience during the final year of their programmes. In other words, there has been a state of coexistence between the instructionally driven classroom-based element and the experientially dominated employment placement. The placement year has symbolised a concern to ground the vocational studies of the student in the realities of the workplace, but this did not signify that the instructional and experiential elements were feeding into each other.

It is the intention of this chapter both to explore a specific experience of doing an Enterprise in Higher Education (EHE) project on generic or core skills for undergraduates and to analyse the placement process of four-year sandwich degree programmes in Business Studies. Crucially, this means that this is an attempt to make sense of the placement process for students *within* a project on developing and assessing generic or core skills. The conclusions were therefore undoubtedly dependent on the project, which shaped and contextualised the attempts to produce data on the nature of the student experience within a placement. The approach to analysing the students' experiences on placement started with a concern for general skills such as problem solving, communication, numeracy, working as part of a team, sometimes referred to as generic or core skills. The project, therefore, did not set out to explore the development of the students in terms of knowledge relevant to academic subjects taught on business degrees, nor did it embark on investigating the intellectual (analytical and creative) skills which might be used in both academic study or practical problem solving. The generic skills which were being considered were likely to be relevant to a range of businesses which undergraduates might enter on completing their degree. However, while a rough plan of what the project should achieve was formulated at the outset, it was not known in advance just what would emerge in terms of a personal development and profiling system. (A profiling system means here any system for capturing data about student attainments in relation to generic skills.)

Business teachers generally know very little about what is being learnt by students on placement. Consequently a methodology for developing profiling must provide data on the placement and space for conceptualising the student learning experience within it. In this particular project a three-stage process was evolved: in the first stage data was to be produced which would enable the project team to begin by discovering what went on in the placement; this was to be followed by experimentation with a model of personal development and profiling; and the third stage was to involve planning what changes were formally required in the programme. The design for the project process is shown on page 70.

The project did result in the successful introduction of profiling into an undergraduate Business Studies programme, but major issues concerning the educational value of the placement, the role of student motivation and self-direction and the capacity of profiling to enhance the placement experience for students were all brought sharply into focus as a result of the project.

In the rest of this chapter the consecutive stages of the project are presented, together with an analysis of the three issues which the work of

Stage	Key questions	Project activity
Discovery	What competences should be/are developed by students on placement?	Researching experiences and perceptions of students, employers and teaching staff.
Experimentation	Is the personal development and profiling system feasible and acceptable?	Piloting the profiling and the personal development with current students and employers and training the academic staff who make the placement visits.
Innovation	Can the personal development and profiling system become an integral and continuously evolving aspect of an undergraduate programme?	Negotiating changes in course regulations, the assessment of the placement (credit rating?) and the role of staff who carry out visits (changing from public relations function to a facilitator and assessor role), and negotiating with resource holders for necessary changes in resources.

Figure 7.1   *The design of the profiling project.*

the project exposed. The conclusion summarises the lessons of this study for the use and value of profiling in relation to placements in undergraduate Business Studies programmes.

Discovery

The EHE project at the Business School of the University of North London ~s not an imposition but an opportunity. There was a history of ⸺ff on the undergraduate Business Studies course evaluating the placement and taking small initiatives to enhance its educational value. Three or four years before the project began there had been ideas about making the placement more integral to the programme. Without EHE support, however, teaching workloads would have kept the desire to improve the placement year peripheral.

The EHE project was also positively motivating: it signalled that someone saw the placement year as sufficiently important that they would put resources into its improvement. Naturally they also expected outcomes from the project. The EHE framework also reinforced reflection: the members of the project team were encouraged to reflect on their work by the EHE system of monitoring and evaluation.

These factors energised the project and made the difference in seeing the placement as having the potential for long-term improvement. Perhaps this can be related to the project team's decision to confront the taken-for-granted nature of the benefits of the placement process. What, they wanted to know, did students learn while on placements? Some of the answers were surprising and sustained the energy within the project team.

During the discovery phase the project team opened itself up to the views and experiences of a wide range of people involved in the placement process. All students on placement and fourth-year students who had just returned from placement were involved in workshops to generate evidence of their perceptions and experiences. Employers were interviewed by academic staff making placement visits. Feedback was also obtained from the placement tutors who visited placement students, and information on the prior anticipations of second-year students was produced.

The fourth-year students produced very useful ideas both on the opportunities and constraints in using placement experiences for learning and personal development and on who needed to be involved in the placement as a learning opportunity. On constraints, they stressed that the placement only lasts for a year, that the organisational setting and mundane jobs into which they are sometimes placed are a disincentive to learning. The fact that, in their view, they are not always given sufficient responsibility is also a disincentive. But a few suggested that students had scope for using their own initiative to improve the placement by being prepared to take responsibility and put themselves forward. In their view, apart from the student, the most critical person to be involved in the placement year was the student's manager in the workplace; teaching staff were mentioned much less often as important in the placement year. Considering the manager's availability to the student on placement, it is not surprising that this person is more important than the academic tutor. This finding underlined the need for a partnership with the employer in the effective use of the placement.

Some 130 students, employers and tutors were involved (as represent-atives of the main stakeholders in the placement) in the production of five separate lists of competences, which were then combined by the project team into a single 'pooled' list. There was a substantial degree of correspondence and overlap between all five lists – with interpersonal skills far exceeding the rest in frequency of being identified.

In retrospect, the project team made good progress at this first discovery stage.

Work-based education?

Unlike the cases of placements in some other vocational programmes, the Business Studies degree placement in many universities involves the suspension of student status and the formal acquisition of employee status. The students support themselves by the salary they receive from their host organisation. This has profound and diverse effects. Some of the students feel that they are being treated entirely the same as regular employees; in other cases the placement consists of special projects, indicating the students' unusual and temporary status as employees. More subtle yet, some students feel themselves being treated simultan-eously as employee and student. Sometimes this works positively for the student, as in cases where the host organisation puts itself out to provide development opportunities for the student because it wishes to contribute to the student's vocational preparation; sometimes the impact is negative – the student on placement gets the worst jobs because they are really 'only' students.

Traditional approaches to business education and work-based learning do not mix easily and the project's discovery stage found some evidence of this. First, students perceived very little of the material covered in the first two years of the degree as relevant or useful in respect of the placement, and what they actually learnt while on placement was not seen as narrowly academic – indeed, first and foremost they seemed to be learning interpersonal skills. Secondly, some students reported that tutors on final-year modules (postplacement) behaved as though the placement year had not existed and made no reference to it in their teaching. Staff welcomed the greater maturity they diagnosed in the 'returners' but, arguably, saw the placement year as character building and a 'good thing' rather than as having a strict educational value. Of course attempts can be made to counter this tendency for the placement and academic learning to coexist but not interact: student debriefing sessions can be attended by all staff (staff hear about the placements from the students, while students have the benefit of a debriefing session); tutors in the pre-placement years can set assignments involving the production of student CVs to be used by placement officers; and programmes can incorporate the marks for a placement report in calculations for determining degree classifications.

But what educational value could a placement have? Within the EHE project the answers to this question were only explored in relation to generic personal competences. Final-year students who had just completed a year of work placement, although they expressed themselves in different ways, nearly all identified the importance of the interpersonal skills they had developed through their work experience. Some mentioned interpersonal skills for dealing with the world at large, dealing with all levels of people and talking to a variety of people; others referred to 'interpersonal communicative adaptability', the ability to interact in the workplace and 'negotiating communication skills'. The students mentioned various other skills (eg applying academic theory, gaining insight into/exposure to a business environment, information technology, confidence/interaction with colleagues, responsibility, and technical skills), but none were re-echoed by them in the same way that interpersonal skills and communication skills were.

The implications of this need to be worked out with some care. There has been a collapse of confidence in the relevance of academic knowledge as a source of progress and power within the business world which has led to a celebration of the natural, spontaneous activity of business practitioners. This strand of thinking rushes in to imitate (and thereby flatter) natural business management practice and language. It assumes that the best business management practice is a style, a superficial appearance, which must be imitated and copied by the business student. Thus, students must be taught how to use the 'discourse' of current natural business practice rather than the stilted and esoteric language of the academic world. In effect, this strand of thinking, in its higher education (HE) manifestation, requires business students to acquire the social skills and the language of the natural business manager, impregnated with the current norms and codes of behaviour of the contemporary business world. The students, then, need to develop the interpersonal skills they appear to be learning on placement.

This is not a solution, however, if the educational value of the placement has not been established. The work of the EHE project team had been aimed at making the placement a more integral part of BA Business Studies. This will only be achieved if the real educational value of the placement experience can be realised.

Thus it is necessary for HE teachers to resist the temptation to rest on the immediate appearance that the placement is simply about the development of interpersonal skills which will help students integrate themselves into business organisations. Looking into this more deeply means looking at the students' placement experiences in terms of concepts which education cherishes (eg intellectual analytical skills) and discovering important educational outcomes which were not expected. Student views of a competence did not always conform to an academic's view of a skill or competence, for example 'confidence' is not usually seen by teachers as a skill. However, education is about the ability and the willingness to learn, and this requires confidence. Or to take another, albeit negative, example, the project team should perhaps have expected to find much on analytical skills. But there were no references by students to the placement developing their ability to evaluate the quality of data or evidence, corroborate observations and conclusions, re-evaluate and reinterpret data and conclusions, identify inconsistencies, recognise their own errors and mistakes, connect evidence and conclusions and so on.

The degree of impact of any intervention into the placement's role in the typical Business Studies degree is ultimately attributable to how well the perceptions of the placement year among teaching staff can be challenged and confronted. Even those involved as champions of change, for example project teams in EHE, may only partially change their perceptions of the placement.

For some teachers placements are periods in which students 'grow up' a bit, thus providing a precondition of maturity for proper study in the final year of the programme. Where this old perception of the chief value of the experience as some hothouse maturation process remains, the possibility and amount of organisational learning about using placements as opportunities for work-based education are curtailed.

Experimenting

The decision to build a pilot phase into the project was well advised, as it would have been a mistake just to research and then design a profiling system.

The project team wanted a system which delivered a process of development of competence – it did not want to end up with just a system of assessment, nor did it want a system in which 'evidence' of competence could be written up at the end. The concept was of a system which would intervene and shape the placement learning experience. The project team called this system the Personal Development Planning Process. Its aim was to 'support the use of the placement as a structured work-based learning opportunity to develop each student's broad personal competences' (project team's working document).

A portfolio was designed which included a list of the generic competences to be developed (Fig. 7.2) and worksheets for the student to complete with their manager during the placement period. The work-sheets were structured on the basis of setting goals and success criteria to inform developmental activities which were to be jointly planned to exploit the work of the student while on placement. The worksheets also

Competences

1. Interpersonal skills (including negotiation, teamwork)
2. Communication skills (presentations, reports, letters, listening etc)
3. Computing/IT (keyboard skills)
4. Confidence
5. Initiative/responsibility/leadership
6. Time management (including time keeping)
7. Problem solving/analytical/ability to learn/decision making
8. Goal setting/self-management
9. Accuracy in working
10. Self-motivation

Figure 7.2 *The generic competences.*

supported evaluation by, and regular follow-up sessions between the student and their manager.

A number of the competences in the piloted process were more of the nature of personality or personal characteristics than narrowly conceived abilities. The project team discussed this issue with some of the students who had put forward such items – they insisted that they were valid competences, and they stood their ground when challenged. There may be something very important in this more integral definition of competences.

The model that was piloted was based on a concept of profiling which gave the students a degree of autonomy. The key device here was the introduction of a notion of 'valued characteristics' (Raven, 1984). This was initially seen by the project team as the missing link between student motivation and competences. It was thought that students should agree some valued styles of behaviour while on placement and then see how the competences could be developed and assessed in relation to them. For example, a student might say that they value adapting to a new job quickly, or they might value getting things done right first time, or finding new ways of doing jobs better. These would be the valued styles of behaviour and a different set of the competences might be related to each of them. So assessment of developing competence would be in relation to styles of behaviour valued by the student (important for their motivation).

This, in broad terms, was the model which was piloted in 1992–3. In February 1993 we launched the personal competence profiling system on an experimental basis with the intention of testing this new approach. Students and staff were briefed on piloting the system in the last half of the placement year; all the employers were sent explanatory letters enlisting their help and the portfolio pack. The feedback from the piloting, while often positive, raised an issue about the feasibility of a model using the concept of valued characteristics.

What is a valued characteristic?

This concept was experimental and the project team members were not sure how well the Personal Development Portfolio would work. In May 1993 a small group of students and employers were invited to discuss with the project team how well the project had gone. The three employers said they supported the initiative and made some helpful comments to improve the scheme. They wanted it simpler and communicated to employers in direct and clear language. They stressed the importance of training the students in how to use the scheme – they saw this as the key to its feasibility. They urged the project team to avoid being 'gimmicky', but considered that many businesses could benefit from involvement because it would help them to become better at supporting the development of their own employees.

The 'valued characteristics' element of the process was confusing to employers. The project team had assumed that generic competences were the valuable abilities and qualities to be developed, but that the development of these would be restricted by student motivation. To put this another way, the production of characteristics valued by EHE (ie the generic competences) would be restricted by characteristics personally valued by the student. One employer's view of the portfolio was that 'the information/instructions given are confusing – it was not very clear what was required of the placement student and myself, eg characteristics and competences are interchangeable.'

The valued characteristics and the generic or personal competences were not interchangeable, but they were certainly meant to interrelate and interact: a particular characteristic valued by a student was to be achieved by the student making use of their existing competences; these competences might be developed to a higher level as they were mobilised to realise the valued characteristic.

Perhaps students found this formal distinction confusing because they had fundamentally accepted that their learning and development on the degree programme was to be testified by the award of a degree. In consequence their desire for the award of a degree was sufficient justification for any learning outcomes, but only to the extent that those learning outcomes were valued in calculating the degree. Thus they had become socialised into a form of education which did not value personal learning goals and which does not produce learning unless it contributes clearly and manifestly to the qualification sought.

The employer response is more difficult to interpret. Perhaps they see skill formation as a self-evident process leading to better performance at work, and thus the question of the ends to be achieved by means of increased generic skills makes little sense to them.

As a result of the pilot the model's notion of 'valued characteristics', a concept which had been seen as vital to allow the diversity of student motivation to be enlisted in making the system of personal development effective, was dropped. The revised model provided a system in which students and their work-based supervisor agreed objectives, success criteria and learning activities. Objective setting as a process was acceptable, possibly because of its role within appraisal systems which operate in relation to manager–subordinate relationships within industry and commerce.

Innovating

The project team designed a set of ideal roles to implement this system. The scale of the change implied by these ideal roles was too big and not incremental enough. The rationale was based on the assumption that the system should involve the students, their line managers in the placement organisations and the university's teaching and specialist staff in the Personal Development Planning Process.

The students were to be responsible for formulating action plans for activities to achieve personal development objectives, and would meet with their line manager in the host organisation to agree personal development objectives, developmental activities and success criteria for the latter. The line managers were generally to act as mentors, giving guidance and counselling support to their placement students with a view to assisting the development of broad personal competences and completion of the portfolio. The students and their managers were, together, to review progress on a regular basis (at least every three months) and to determine the evidence to be presented that personal development objectives have been achieved. The staff who had formerly only carried out placement visits and marked the placement report were to become assessment tutors. They were to be responsible for acting as consultants to the line managers and students on the programme, helping them to resolve any problems in setting personal development objectives and success criteria; they were to formally assess the students' completed Personal Development Portfolio and provide systematic and detailed feedback to students. Other supporting activities were also to be carried out by these assessment tutors and other academic staff.

The innovation stage was the problematic one for this project. The new system of personal development, using profiling, was attractive and quite acceptable as an aid to personal development on the placement. But the shift to the new roles was only partially achieved. Most crucially, the innovation stopped short in terms of achieving that breakthrough, which would have meant that staff, students and employers saw the placement as an *educational* experience which was valued in the usual currency of the academic world. The students were still not to get credit for a year spent in work-based learning and the assessment of the placement report and the portfolio was to make only a marginal contribution to the determination of the students' degree classifications.

Although the team invested time in project management, it still underestimated the time and effort required for the second and third stages. The greatest strength of the approach adopted was the cohesiveness and commitment of the project team; the greatest weakness was mobilising awareness of the placement issue among the rest of the academic staff. Because others did not participate directly in the discovery stage (and probably would not have wanted to if invited), they were not persuaded of the importance of the need to rethink the placement experience.

At the end of the project in 1993 there were many issues remaining; issues which the EHE project made visible, but did not solve. Should there be a single common profiling system for the university, or should different programmes develop their own, specific systems? Should the portfolio be designed with formative or summative assessment in mind (and thus what about the placement and credit accumulation and transfer systems)? Should the placement just concentrate on personal and transferable skills, or can learning in the workplace be credited in relation to subject/academic knowledge too? These are all serious dilemmas. There is a sense in which they will only be resolved when higher education decides its strategic posture: is it going to conduct its placements as vehicles for imitating the natural business world's skills and language (and seek to keep the placement at arm's length in terms of academic credits), or will it push on even further with the idea of valuing in educational terms learning occurring on the placement?

Imitation and interaction models of profiling

There are great difficulties in finding placements – any placements. These can, however, be overcome through the effective systems of dedicated industrial liaison officers who find placements. Higher education has tried to shape the behaviour of supervisors in the host businesses, traditionally by negotiating with them over the work assignments they give to students. These negotiations take place when teachers make their brief and infrequent placement visits, but also by means of handbooks and booklets sent to influence the employers' perceptions, expectations and behaviour.

Rightly or wrongly, higher education has traditionally assumed pessimistically that most employers are not able or willing to do much more than provide a job, and that teachers therefore have little ability to involve the employer in the educational process.

This pessimism affects not only the construction of the placement experience but also the form of assessment usually favoured for Business Studies placements. Many business schools have traditionally assessed the placement by means of a placement report. This makes minimal demands on students and employers. The report is usually done towards the end of the placement, too late to affect any experience of the placement itself.

This pessimism also affects the possibilities of changing and improving the placement experience. The implications of this are significant both for how change is made and for the kind of profiling system which emerges. At least two options or models of profiling are evident in the case of business undergraduates on placement: the imitation model and the interaction model. Pessimism leads to the imitation model.

Thus the imitation model of profiling jumps to a set of competences and does not bother to research and experiment with them in relation to the specific programme. The competences are the conventional wisdom of the business world – they are obvious and do not need to be researched since they are grounded in acceptability to employers. This is innovation with a closed mind. Such a profiling system based on the pro forma is completed by students reflecting on their placement and ex post facto, students selecting bits of experience to associate with each competence on the list.

In contrast, the interaction model seeks to enable students to participate actively in the development process and to discover and test for themselves their competences, it is based on valid research into the particular competences relevant to business undergraduates and it seeks to ground the competences in the needs of the students, which are different according to the programme area and other local factors. It expects diversity and difference, not universal competences. The interaction model, in our view, implies that students will be empowered to work with line managers to select learning activities, will review the resultant experiences and, together with the line manager, will select evidence relevant to the portfolio.

The interaction model at work

A student in the pilot project wrote to the placement officer:

'The idea of the portfolio is a very good one, I certainly noticed that – instead of solely reviewing the progress of my project – we reviewed my personal progress a lot more and this in turn helped me during the following phases of my project.'

Significantly, therefore, the interaction model of profiling requires a process in which students and line managers plan learning experiences (and thus *form* the learning experiences), thereby actively influencing the *generation* of evidence as an important stage. It allows the selection of evidence to proceed reflectively. The imitation model, which is really uninterested in the learning activities in substantive terms, only allows a selection stage after the 'natural' occurrence of the placement. The placement experience is thus left intact and not enhanced by the imitation model. In a sense, the interaction model is seeking to enrich work experience by *consciously making* the placement a learning experience. The imitation model is only concerned with the assessment aspect and thus is constrained to seeking to allow the students to recognise their experience in the language code of the business world (the language of competences and skills). The implication of the imitation model, then, is to 'allow' academics to continue their real business of teaching students the academic knowledge. Everything changes, and yet nothing changes fundamentally.

Conclusions

In this chapter we have analysed an EHE team's experiences of a project carried out in 1992–3. The aim was to develop the employment placement of business undergraduates into a structured opportunity for students to practise and enhance their personal management skills through the use of a profiling system. Looking at this experience we find:

- a lot of evidence of the non-involvement of teachers in the placement *as a learning experience for students*;
- the problem of generating *awareness* among subject specialists in the teaching team of the issue of placement as a work-based learning opportunity;
- the way in which the project led to us *revising* our view of this opportunity as a small, hardly noticeable issue into one of major importance for the development of Business Studies degrees.

The chapter has described the characteristics of the placement year in business degree courses, the main stages of the project to design a model of profiling for personal development purposes and, finally, the consequences flowing from developing the placement year as an educational experience.

The most important point this chapter has made is the need to establish a real partnership with employers in planning, using and exploiting the placement as an educational experience. The temptation to categorise the placement in non-educational terms is great. This is the result of seeing the qualities and the language of the natural world as merely a garb in which to clothe business students, and the placement as merely a 'restyling' process. This allows the old separation – the non-involvement of higher education in business – to persist.

The elitism and indifference of the traditional business degree was not just a symptom of the relation between education and practice; it was also a manifestation of the curriculum within education. Academic subjects were transmitted to students to be memorised. Students were not enabled to participate in the learning process by discovering and testing ideas. They were there to be fed knowledge. Their problem of ignorance was to be solved by academics giving them bodies of knowledge. Student complaints about such systems of education of course surfaced in the 1960s. But the practice of this traditional type of education is far from extinct, which leads us to define another response to the crisis of traditional business education.

This is to design educational courses which enable students to discover and actively participate in learning, leading to higher value educational outcomes. The ability and willingness to learn can only be built by experiences which require these things, and to require things is, in the educational world, to assess them and use them in determining the degree classification. This is not a recipe for softness and indulgence to students; it is a choice which implies registering even higher expectations and demands on the students. This will not merely be a restyling job with the old practices preserved underneath.

Reference

Raven, J (1984) *Competence in Modern Society*, H K Lewis, London.

Chapter 8

Profiling Transferable Skills in the Social Sciences

David Taylor

Introduction

Profiling of transferable skills was introduced on the modular BSc Applied Social Science degree scheme (SSS) over a period of three years. The SSS consists of seven named interdisciplinary degree routes with approximately 175 modules offered at preliminary, intermediate and final level. Several profile formats were discussed and piloted with staff and students and a final version introduced for students at preliminary level in 1994–5. Intermediate and final levels will be covered by the profile from 1995–6. The profile operates at the 'programme' level and therefore stands apart from the direct delivery of individual modules. The development of the profile has involved extensive discussions about underlying aims and philosophy, operational principles, implementation strategies and evaluation among staff, students and employers. The following discussion outlines the background to and implementation of the profile.

Background

During the initial discussions of the aims of profiling in the Social Sciences an early decision was taken to avoid a focus on behavioural competence such as that adopted by the National Council for Vocational Qualifications (NCVQ). Such a focus was rejected for both pragmatic and philosophical reasons. In the first instance there was no identifiable lead body or specific employment area from which to derive appropriate competence, and secondly, and more fundamentally, the behaviourist focus of functional analysis and of the competence movement in general seemed inappropriate for the development of higher order transferable intellectual skills. Such approaches tend to employ a false dichotomy between skills and knowledge where both are analytically separated and knowledge relegated to an 'underpinning' platform upon which behavioural performance rests. The approach employed in this project sees knowledge and skill as two aspects of the same process in which 'performance' is reflexive, adaptive and intellectual as much as behavioural. The aim of the profile is therefore to develop reflexive autonomous learning rather than performance according to externally derived indicators. The profile does not attempt to deliver the skills but to enable learners to identify and monitor their skills development.

Profiling principles

Avoiding the 'performance according to specification' model of competence and focusing on reflexive learning led to the view that the profile should be:

- formative rather than summative;
- non-assessed;
- developmental (ie capable of adaptation during use); and
- generic (ie capable of being employed across a range of 'learning contexts').

Formative v summative profiling

In line with wider institutional policy the SSS project adopted a view of profiling as a *process* rather than a *product*. The main aim, therefore, has been to help students identify, monitor and plan their own skill development. The implicitly summative statement of skills acquired in the full profile is seen as less important than the development of a student's ability to identify, plan, adapt, take responsibility for, reflect upon and present in a variety of contexts to others, a range of specific and transferable skills. The formative role of the profile in guiding learning is therefore central.

Non-assessed

Given the formative role of the profile, it was felt it should act as a facilitative mechanism and stand apart from the formal assessment process. Concern was raised that assessing personal and interpersonal skills could easily become an evaluation of personality. Commitment to this approach was strong but proved to be one of the key areas of debate during the implementation stage (see below for further discussion of implementation issues). The questions of verification and evidence were contentious among the wider staff group and problems of student commitment were raised if the 'stick' of assessment was removed. The latter problem is overcome by the use made of the skills statement as a basis for completion of an end-of-year personal reference record. The completion of the profile thus enables a fuller reference based on a deeper knowledge of an individual student's skills.

Developmental

The idea that the format should allow for diversity of use and interpretation was also felt to be key. Having rejected the idea of fixed competence based on behavioural performance, part of the profile was left open ended to allow students to identify whatever skills they themselves felt appropriate and to suggest ways these could be demonstrated. This approach goes some way to recognising the differential access to opportunities for skills development due to discrimination; values non-traditional forms of learning and skills acquisition and avoids the overly 'ablist' assumptions of many behaviourally derived performance indicators.

Genericism

While most attention within the profiling system is paid to skills acquisition within the taught curriculum, the implications of the principles outlined above were that a wide range of 'learning contexts' should be included within the profile. Six 'learning contexts' from which students could bring evidence of skills development were identified:

1. the taught curriculum;
2. college-based practical work;
3. practical fieldwork;
4. placements;
5. prior certified learning;
6. prior and contemporary experiential learning.

The last category is not limited to work-based learning but includes voluntary work and domestic life-course learning.

Operational principles

The profile operates as a two-stage process. The first stage is concerned with allowing students to identify their current level of skills development across a wide range of skills fields. This raises a number of issues. The profiling activity may be the first time students have made a *self-assessment* of their own level of development. Any assessment which involves the attachment of value to a process of product of learning can be seen as having a number of elements.

1. What is being assessed must be clearly understood and defined (this not only raises the issue of what exactly is meant by a particular skill designation but also its meaning for the student making an assessment).
2. The criteria to be used in making an assessment should be clearly understood (students may not be clear on what basis to make a judgement).
3. The basis on which values are attached to criteria – are they absolute and 'criterion referenced', or normative – needs to be explicit.

In this respect students may find a difficulty in deciding whether to apply what they believe to be some absolute measure, or whether to relate their own skill level to that of their perception of their peers. In order to address some of these problems strategies of self- and peer-assessment have been introduced into a number of taught modules within the SSS and integrated into the delivery of the subject. Thus the profile can be seen as interrelated with the curriculum. When using the self-assessment questionnaire (see below) these issues of assessment are discussed with the tutor and explored in student workshops.

The second stage consists of students making a skills statement comprising a description of the skill including reference to the criteria used to define it; an account of the learning context(s) in which it was developed and has been applied, indicating the evidence of its successful use; and lastly, in conjunction with a tutor, a statement about any further aspects of the skill which could be developed or other opportunities for applying it. The philosophy here has been that in order to profile skills learners must first become aware of how to identify and assess them.

Profile format

Self-assessment questionnaire

In order to achieve the above a Self-assessment Skills Questionnaire was developed based on work done by Lynne Thorley at Hertfordshire University and similar work at a range of other institutions. Skills were broken down into four 'fields'; communication and information skills; personal and interpersonal skills; intellectual skills; organisational skills. This somewhat arbitrary classification was helpful in focusing attention on different types and levels of skills, but its value as a formal taxonomy is very limited. In the current profile, adapted after piloting, communication and information skills have been separated into two distinct fields.

Within the original four fields a total of 31 skills were listed and space was left for other skills which students themselves wished to identify (see Operational principles, above). In addition to the skills listing a two-stage value scale was used in the first version of the questionnaire. In stage one students were asked to identify their current level on all skills listed, and in stage two they were asked to identify the importance of each skill to them in the context of their own academic programme and further educational and career plans. In both stages a six-point rating scale was used from 'high' (six) to 'low' (one). The comparison between the first and second scores was meant to allow students to focus on and plan for further skills development. A problem encountered during the piloting process was that students tended to rate all skills as highly important to their future career plans. In the final profile the second stage ranking was removed and the identification of a personal development plan became part of a more general discussion process with the tutor.

The following are indicative examples of the skills descriptions from the different fields covered by the questionnaire:

- Communication skills (example). Oral presentations: the ability to present ideas orally to an audience and to discuss and argue a case.
- Information skills (example). Information seeking: the ability to seek, store and retrieve information by a variety of methods.
- Personal and interpersonal skills (example). Group/team work: the ability to cooperate with others on a variety of roles and to achieve individual and group tasks.
- Intellectual skills (example). Critical and analytical thinking: ability to consider issues from a range of perspectives, to understand them and draw on appropriate concepts and values in arriving at a critical assessment of them.
- Organisational skills (example). Planning skills: ability to make and carry through an action plan, individually or with others, to achieve a given objective.

Skills profile

The second element of the profiling process is the skills statement itself. Having reached the stage where a student feels able to make a statement about the level of skill acquired, a two-sided A4 form is completed consisting of three blank boxes:

1. the description of the skill itself;
2. the learning contexts in which it was acquired and the appropriate evidence;

3. the joint statement between student and tutor on aspects of the skill for further development.

Students accumulate a number of such statements which are collated by them in a skills folder over the course of their academic programme.

Operational procedure

An early decision was taken to locate the profile within the personal tutorial system rather than with subject tutors. However, in the early stages of implementation it became apparent that the increasing strains upon the personal tutorial system meant that so much depended upon the individual commitment of tutors and the motivation of students that its operation was uneven. In the current, revised, procedure specific profiling dates are timetabled in which personal tutors meet students in group workshops with structured tasks, undertaken in student pairs. Initial self-assessments take place once in each semester, with follow-up sessions devoted to discussions of the subsequent skills statements.

Relationship to curriculum

As already noted, the profile stands apart from the curriculum. However, all taught modules within the SSS specify learning outcomes, and increasingly these are presented to include a range of transferable skills appropriate to the particular curriculum. This provides a resource for students not only within the curriculum but as a base upon which to draw when considering current skills acquisition and in planning future development through the choice of modules. Additionally students on particular degree pathways are exposed to different forms of skills learning. For example, the four-year Social Research pathway includes a one-year research placement in which students negotiate a skills-based learning contract with their agency supervisor. This helps foster an atmosphere in which skills are centrally located in the whole learning process.

Implementation

The original profiling system was drawn up by a small working group as part of the Enterprise in Higher Education (EHE) initiative. A number of wider staff development sessions were held subsequently where initial enthusiasm was strong. However, in the first year of implementation tutorial staff varied in their commitment to the process. This was predominantly a result of attempting to locate the profiling process within the traditional tutorial system which itself is increasingly under strain. In fact issues of timetabling and resources emerged as a key factor in the potential success of the project. Subsequently profiling activity was entered on staff timetables and hours formally allocated. Additionally, designated times have been indicated on student timetables for profiling, thus formalising the process.

A second key factor in ensuring staff commitment has been the emphasis on the higher level transferable skills and the avoidance of the competence model alluded to earlier. In a Social Science context, albeit one which emphasises interdisciplinarity, the essentially contested nature of knowledge and the related need for a range of intellectual skills which facilitate transference, comparison and critical evaluation avoid the charge of vocational instrumentalism.

The question of evidence and the status of the profile, especially given the decision that it should be non-assessed, was raised during the early stages of implementation. Some staff were concerned that the student statement relied on 'testimony' which could not always be verified, especially if the learning had taken place in a context other than the curriculum, and without formal assessment its value outside the university would be limited. The central aim, however, has been to foster the *process* of profiling, and other measures outside the profile address the validity of skills statements. Students are expected to consider what counts as evidence and to offer what they see as verification, which may not always be formally accredited.

A particular, and important, implementation issue has been the difficulty of operating a programme-wide system with part-time students. Two factors are especially relevant here: first, difficulty of access to students who may have very restricted availability and, secondly, the problem of adequate resources to commit personal tutors to part-time students. This problem is being further considered in the next stage of development.

Advantages and constraints

While the increased emphasis on skills-based learning outcomes gives a clearer understanding to students of curriculum focus, these can still be rather impersonal. The process of profiling, based as it is on the development of personal skills founded upon a self-assessment, allows a more personal account of a learner's achievements. To the extent that it enables students to recognise and develop personal skills it can boost self-confidence and broaden self-perception.

The identification of current skills level and areas for development helps students monitor their own progress and is an important dimension in the development of autonomous learning. It aids the process of programme planning and of future career planning. Additionally, the final profile document is a useful resource to students when making job, research or other postcompletion applications.

Operating at the programme level, rather than being integrated into specific module delivery, can also bring a sense of integration to a modular programme. However, a difficulty of operating at this level is maintaining a diversity of skills opportunities in the context of wide student choice of modules.

As already noted, one constraint can be the commitment of staff, if adequate provision is not made to indicate profiling as a central part of the delivery of the academic programme. This is helped where formal, timetabled resources are committed.

Conclusion

The aim of the SSS profile is to foster the skills of critical judgement and the ability to transfer knowledge and skills across cognitive domains and social contexts. It aims to challenge the distinction between skills and knowledge and emphasise skills acquisition as a dynamic process of adaptation and application. The SSS profile is a first stage in the process of breaking down the knowledge/skills divide characterised by performance-based measures of competence.

Chapter 9

Film Studies' Record of Achievements

K MacKinnon

During the autumn term of 1991/2, in the very first months of the University of North London's five-year initiative in Enterprise in Higher Education (EHE), a principal area of discussion among managers and faculty coordinators of the project was 'profiling'. I was coordinator for the Faculty of Humanities and Teacher Education between 1991 and 1993, the remaining 50 per cent of my timetable being devoted to the area of Film Studies, of which I have been full-time (day) subject tutor since its inception in 1984.

Background

Rapid headway seemed to be made in team discussions through the examination of several competing (or complementary) models of profile. An example of this headway is that we enunciated some guiding principles: we were against the completion of exhaustive checklists, but *for* student 'ownership' of the profiles. We were not impressed by the need to dwell on the inevitable negative aspects of any student's experience, but were impressed by the attractions of leaving it to the student, having decided which aspects to pick as positive, to indicate why. We became sensitive to the connotations of certain language, preferring for instance 'Record of Achievements' to 'Profile' in the belief that the former more clearly stressed the positive.

Keen to move away from the abstract and principled, once that necessary stage had been reached by the team, I wanted to see whether Film Studies could produce its own version of a Record of Achievements. Film Studies was, after all, at that time unique among humanities subjects in that it had a tradition of evaluating students' seminar work (10 per cent of most taught unit assessment marks then, 20 per cent now) and of encouraging cooperation through group work, moving the emphasis away from individual 'performance' and rewarding, say, good listening as well as useful contributions of the more generally recognised sorts. It seemed likely that staff interest not only in fostering group work and attitudes of responsibility to others in sub-groups, but in encouraging student awareness of the process of seminar planning and running, would prove relevant. Employment beyond the degree course could well involve, for example, the ability to give and take in small group discussion and to realise where behaviour helps or hinders useful results emerging from such discussion. (At a conference on the European Dimension which I attended as the institution's EHE representative, one speaker who had conducted research on multinational employer attitudes found that cooperativeness was given a far higher value than individualism in the context of desirable attributes for applicants.)

Planning

Towards the end of 1991 full-time Film Studies staff began regular discussions of what we hoped would be a practicable Record of Achievements. We were aware that Film Studies is much misunderstood both within academia and, certainly, beyond it. Therefore one of the first decisions was to write an account of our subject's aims and methods, to show that students who do well with us can turn their hands to a surprising variety of other pursuits, with experience that is relevant. Initially we felt that students could send this to a prospective employer, for example, but we later decided against that advice, believing it more important for students to realise that they dare not assume knowledge of their education; that if they do not address the question of absent (or false) information they could be letting themselves down badly.

We considered our course in terms of what most contributed to the notion of transferable skills, and decided to concentrate on – apart from the crucial matter of the seminars – the practice/theory unit and the final-year project. We then tried to consider what relevant claims could be made about the study of the subject in general. Aware that different

students had different aptitudes and approaches, we drew up lists of potential achievements for various areas under such headings as 'Student responsibility', 'Personal qualities', 'Transferable skills', trying hard to avoid the sorts of confusing debates about significations of nomenclature which could be more vital to specialists in EHE.

It seemed fair that, if students were to feel student ownership was a reality, they should decide for themselves which strengths they could claim. At the same time we felt that there had to be a check on over-optimistic accounts or, more importantly, that there had to be an affirmation of credible claims from the staff's knowledge of the individual student over the course. We decided, therefore, that:

1. students would first choose what to write about themselves, under which headings;
2. they would then consult with personal tutors to discuss their drafts;
3. staff would either write in asseverative comments, with 'evidence' where appropriate, or advise students to rewrite, by additions or deletions, in order to have credible support offered by the teachers.

Because by this stage we could see that students left on their own to complete a Record might be puzzled as to the point, we drew up a statement from us to students, covering such questions as 'Why is a Record of Achievements important?' We felt, too, that we should ask finalists to undertake the completion of the Record and that we should meet them in a group initially to listen to objections or questions.

Testing opinion

A number of student volunteers were asked to consider the proposed Record of Achievements, its methodology and the suggestions for its accomplishment. Students are generally so busy, however (by the time they have sufficient awareness of the subject and their part in it to make valuable contributions), that they cannot be expected to devote sufficient time to the proposals even in draft form for us to feel confident that these have been considered in detail. (An ideal way of formulating proposals would have been to have had student representatives participating in all our discussions, but it was clear from the subject Boards of Studies at which we requested such participation that this was not going to be practicable.)

We expected questioning of the point of the exercise, since, however neatly we had packaged the Record and its documentation – even to the extent of providing sheets for completion and a fictitious 'student statement' as possible inspiration – it clearly demanded *some* time and a fair degree of concentration. This was not what students questioned, in the main. Largely they appreciated that they needed, for whatever future they had in mind, to reflect on and to understand their various successes, both in terms of 'personal development' as well as in those of growing academic competence and confidence.

We did, however, find that what we believed to be admirably clear and concise explanations to students did not prevent them from being, in some cases, mystified by 'what we wanted'. What we believed to be our sincere wish, that students 'owned' the Record, was not fully credited by the volunteers, who felt that we must want certain responses and not others. (To an extent, this was a justified suspicion, since why else would we affirm some claims and not others?)

We quickly learned, if we referred them to the explanatory Notes for Students section, that these had been skimmed or left aside. Nobody claimed that they were unhelpful or opaque. Instead we had to accept that students under pressure chose to concentrate on the central sections, and placed more value on a question-and-answer method of clarification than the printed guide in which we had placed our faith. This suggested, unless our sample was atypical of future students, that we had to give greater attention to the need to spend time with students when first they were presented with the documentation.

When the university's 'pioneer profile' was presented to the EHE team it was both enthusiastic and encouraging, one coordinator immediately announcing that he intended to adapt it to the needs of his more ambitious faculty-wide version. Concern was felt, though, particularly by the representative of the Careers Service, that it was too late to introduce the Record, however admirable in itself, at final-level stage. While it was accepted that students had the breadth of vision at that point to complete the Record with some confidence, it was felt that there had to be more concern with the building of an 'ethos' – of which the Record of Achievements would be a natural culmination rather than a new departure at the last stages of film study. Once again, the subject staff were thus made conscious of the demands on them in terms of that most precious and scarce of resources – time. Both students and specialist staff had pointed to the need to devote more hours than we felt we could allow for, not just to the clarification of the Record but to that of the subject's EHE project in general, the embedding of EHE relevance within the subject from the students' early days.

It had been even more difficult to gain employer than student help with the evolution of the Record of Achievements. Humanities has a particular problem when it comes to the identification of 'likely' employers, since it is in the nature of humanities subjects and that of the world beyond that the relations between them will be unpredictable and oblique. That is, humanities equips students with a range of transferable skills and confidence in their articulacy and intelligence which means that they ought to be strong contenders in the context of employment opportunities. What it does not do is point successful graduates towards a clear set of employments, as more vocational courses might be expected to do.

Much of our energy in the design of the Record went towards the students' verbalisation of what was undoubtedly true of them but of what is often, disastrously, unstated by them – that their achievements range far beyond competence and sometimes brilliance in their chosen fields of study. Clearly this priority and the tactics for its achievement needed consideration by employers.

The best opportunity for an exchange of views proved to be at a special employers' event arranged by the managers of the EHE project in May 1992, and at which I offered an account of the Record's formulation. More importantly, students who had taken part in the experimental period spoke eloquently, and without undue loyalty to the proposers, of the value which they perceived in the initiative. The invited employers seemed interested and indeed enthusiastic about what could be expected to emerge. One pointed out that what might be a strength in a Social Services application could still be a weakness in a different sort of application. (By that stage, we were becoming clearer in any case that the Record would be retained by the student for future use – not to be sent as it stood, but to be built on and adapted in the light of particular demands.)

Another useful opportunity was afforded by the invitation to me to present the ideas and documentation to the EHE Steering Committee, at which, for example, representatives from the Training, Enterprise and Education Directorate (TEED) could consider the plan's merits and pitfalls with me. In the event the strongest encouragement came from that source, although they also believed that the project would probably need a greater input of staff time than might appear to have been planned for. By this stage (the second year of the university's EHE project), a paper had been submitted by its management to the Academic Quality Committee, making the point that the university's commitment to EHE initiatives would demand a husbanding of its resources, especially in the years after the five-year period had ended.

Experience, 1992–4

Part of the concept of student ownership of the Record of Achievements must be acceptance that, with whatever encouragement, some students will choose not to go through the process of consultation and completion, and 1993–4 was depressing in this particular respect since extremely few of even the 'good', motivated students so chose. It has to be said, however, that the year was highly atypical. There was a prolonged student occupation of the faculty's Kentish Town precinct in May which required considerable rescheduling of some examinations and which, even for subjects such as ours which do not examine, produced record cases of absent coursework even at 'resit' stage in September. Previous years have been more encouraging.

Students seldom need to be 'converted' to the notion of the value of this undertaking. Some have already had difficulties in presenting themselves in writing or interview and leap at the chance of gaining practice in so doing. An unexpected bonus in the 'affirmation' element of the process is that students seem genuinely surprised and heartened by seeing how minutely we observe their virtues and the occasions on which these were particularly demonstrated. Perhaps staff praise for students tends otherwise to be relegated to confidential references or examination boards. Students who read and then can retain positive assessments of their claims seem much inspired to know that we have a real appreciation of them.

We generally have more vocal enthusiasts at the initial meetings than we have completed Records of Achievement. The pressure of work seems to deplete the numbers, particularly in the case of 'less committed' students, who may nevertheless have special need of the chance to form judgements of their careers with us. This defect seems once again to point to the need for greater input in the form of staff–student discussion than we have been able to find time for, and may bear out the point from Careers about building up an ethos, and therefore a sense of 'normal expectation'.

Some tentative conclusions

Specifically, there is an as yet unresolved problem within the institution (and thus within this faculty and subject area) concerning the resourcing of otherwise laudable EHE activities. In a time of diminishing resources (relative to the growing claims on academic staff time, that is), space has to be found in a crowded calendar for the fostering of positive attitudes. These in turn need to be based on a willingness to consider and discuss sceptical responses through, for example, frank exchanges of views and answering of even hostile questions. These questions could be expected from students who are less aware than they might ideally be of the point of EHE activities, but are also asked by colleagues, particularly those who have not yet participated in the planning of an EHE project.

The humanities scheme, of which Film Studies forms only a small part, is itself devising a 'profile' which may be completed by the end of the academic year 1994–5. The relation of similar subject initiatives to a scheme profile will have to be considered, and the questions of time (resources and timing in a more general sense) will have to be entered into with more vigour than hitherto. (While the need to secure resources

UNIVERSITY OF NORTH LONDON

RECORD OF ACHIEVEMENTS
BA (Hons) Humanities

Name ....   Date ..29 / 1 / 93..............

Student Statement on Personal Quality: ...FLEXIBILITY...

Flexibility was not easy for me, as a mature student, to acquire. The seminar
experience is hardly ever the same twice and a student has to be flexible and adapt.
One has to be alert to visual, written and verbal information that may be
communicated through role-playing, debate, brainstorming or questionnaire formats. I
have found that a flexibility towards new and different methods of learning is
invaluable.

Staff Comment

Martin has shown dexterity in handling the variety of assignments, and their
associated techniques, required of Film students. He has clearly grown in confidence
and adaptability, so that what he was potentially capable of has now been
impressively actualised.

J. Kennedy MacKinnon   2/2/93

Student Statement on Personal Quality: RESPONSIBILITY.........................

Assuming responsibility for a BA (Honours) degree has been a learning experience in
itself. But more than responsibility for myself and my work I've developed a sense
towards others through working closely in small groups towards given objectives, with
each member of the group assigned a role which must be performed and further
collective responsibility for the task in hand. Assuming responsibility in these
situations has also allowed me opportunities to overcome shyness in seminar debates
and promoted my self-confidence in dealing with people that I don't know but must
forge a working relationship with.

Staff Comment

Martin's seminar performance has been exemplary since he gained the confidence to
participate fully. He was always a good listener, but he made obvious gains through
role-play in one seminar and went beyond the call of duty to keep a seminar that was
in dire trouble, through no fault of his own, going. He has developed noticeably in
his organisational ability, handling peers tactfu;lly but persuasively.   JKM 2/2/93

Continuation sheet

Student Statement on Personal Quality: *SELF — DISCIPLINE*

Successfully completing a three year full-time degree course has proved invaluable in promoting my self-discipline. Maintaining a good attendance record, producing written work to strict deadlines and structuring my free time in order to balance my studies with my home life, so that neither suffered unduly, has not always proved easy but I have accomplished it and take some pride in the fact.

Staff Comment

He has proved exemplary in regularity of class attendance, in time-keeping both with regard to the submission of assignments and to full participation in lectures, screenings and seminars, as well as in the merit of the work undertaken – and all this from the comparatively long distance of Brighton.

JKM   2/2/93

Student Statement on Personal Quality: *COMMUNICATION*

An ability to communicate orally with people is a skill which I gained through work experience and brought with me to college. What I have consciously nurtured during my academic studies is the ability to communicate information and ideas both clearly and effectively through my written work. Communication being a two-way thing, I have also learned to listen to information given and assess a task accordingly so that my assignments reflect this assimilated information.

Staff Comment

There has already been favourable comment on his listening – not just in terms of attentiveness but in intelligence and pertinence of response. He can be relied on to take a full part in team work and to help and encourage others with unfailing good humour. While self-deprecating, he gains his way by powers of persuasion.

JKM   2/2/93

Figure 9.1   *Example of a Record of Achievements.*

for EHE work is obvious, the danger within the institution is that these resources may seem to be taken, in a finite pool, from areas in real need of them, so that EHE is perceived as a threat to, rather than an adjunct of, 'academic' work.)

More generally I feel that there are implications for 'academic' work from EHE. It is obviously far easier to construct a Record that can lay claim to the acquisition of transferable skills in a subject context, where concern is felt for the encouragement of awareness of process and for the development of the student not simply as passive learner but as active participant. The brighter side of this is that the situation is fluid. Understanding of the relevance of profiling, both to hardheaded matters of employment and to a sense of personal achievement in study, seems likely to lead to an awareness of the relevance of the curriculum and especially of its 'delivery'.

Being in at the beginning of things, in institutional terms, has its drawbacks, not the least of which is that enthusiasm, particularly when the results are imperfect, can be characterised as naive or even sweetly ingenuous – which has its own effect on the initial enthusiasm that pioneered the Record of Achievements. Yet the satisfactions to be gained at the beginning of any significant development are obvious.

Chapter 10

Profiling the Year Abroad in Modern Language Degrees

M Dueñas-Tancred and I Weber-Newth

Introduction

Students on Modern Language degrees at the University of North London, as in most institutions of higher education, are required to spend their third year in a country where their chosen language is spoken. The aim of this year abroad is to improve the students' linguistic competence and to provide the opportunity for them to experience the foreign culture. As year abroad tutors we are aware that students gain much more from their year abroad than just academic development. Colleagues comment on how students have matured and how their confidence has increased when they return for their fourth year. This impression corresponds with the students' own judgement of what they have gained during this year. In order to acknowledge and assess the importance of the non-academic learning we have developed a profiling system for the year abroad. Pilot projects confirmed, furthermore, that profiling not only records the students' progress but can also foster the development of transferable skills. Profiling now forms an integral part of the course structure of our Modern Language degrees as a component of the year abroad.

Course structure of Modern Language degrees

At the University of North London students in the School of Languages and European Studies can study French, German, Spanish, Italian or Russian. They study these subjects either within the Humanities scheme or within the European Studies scheme. In either of these schemes the course lasts four years. Students in the Humanities scheme have the option of spending the third year or year abroad either at a university or in a placement as a teaching assistant in a country where the target language is spoken. European Studies students must spend the year at a foreign university.

The student population at the University of North London is heterogeneous: as an innercity university we attract students from a variety of different social and cultural backgrounds. A high proportion of our students come from local ethnic communities. As a consequence of the university's access policy we also teach a wide range of students from different age groups who come to us with a variety of entry qualifications. Students can, therefore, start to study a foreign language at three different entrance levels: as absolute beginners, at an intermediate level or at post A level or equivalent standard. For the first two years the hourly input of language teaching differs according to the initial language level. After successful completion of the second year students should be sufficiently linguistically prepared to spend the third year abroad. This year plays an important role in equalising the spectrum of students' initial entrance levels before they return to their final year.

The School of Languages and European Studies places students in universities in Belgium, France and Martinique for French, Austria, Germany and Switzerland for German, Argentina, Cuba, Ecuador, Mexico, Venezuela and Spain for Spanish. Language students go on placements either within the framework of bilateral agreements between the University of North London and the foreign universities or, increasingly, within the framework of ERASMUS links.

The year abroad

In the Department of Languages and European Studies the year abroad has been an integral part of the language courses for several years. In the past students spent this year with very little guidance or monitoring, often making their own arrangements to study. In many universities this is still the case. The *Independent* (21/4/1994) quoted a University of Cambridge language student as saying: 'Once you are out there you really are left on your own. We were given a college contact number, but it was made clear that this was only for emergencies.' A University College London student says he received no support during his time in

Marseilles. 'UCL didn't even drop me a note to ask how I was getting on.' There have been various articles in the press telling how lost students can feel during their year abroad.

As year abroad tutors we realise that some students are able and motivated enough to benefit fully from the year abroad without preparation or monitoring. Many students, however, floundered, unable to focus on any goals. For this reason students from our department currently embarking on their year abroad are generally well briefed and prepared for the experience. Apart from language classes, they receive information about the different educational structures, cultures and values of the countries where they will be studying. Once abroad they are closely monitored by the year abroad tutor and usually by a responsible colleague at the host university. Most students are also visited by the year abroad tutor during their placement. During this visit students' academic and personal progress are reviewed as part of the profiling system.

The introduction of profiling as a component of the course structure of language degrees was directly linked to the credit rating of the year abroad. While all year abroad placements carry a mandatory grant, they were not previously fully credit rated within the University Common Regulatory Framework. The low weighting of the year abroad did not reflect the important learning that takes place during that period. Taking this into account and following the recommendation of the Standing Conference of Heads of Modern Language Departments' Working Party on the Year Abroad (October 1991) we have given the year abroad a full credit rating of 120 points, the same credit rating as each of the three years spent at the home institution. Half the credits are given to academic work; the other half are accounted for by the concurrent experiential learning which takes place during the year abroad and which is attested in the profile. Whereas all of these components of the year abroad are credited, only the dissertation receives a grade which affects the overall degree classification of the student. The profile itself does not receive a grade.

The four-year Honours degree course has 480 credit points which are divided as follows:

- Year 1: 120 credit points (8 units or modules);
- Year 2: 120 credit points (8 units or modules);
- Year 3: 120 credit points for academic and non-academic development;
- Year 4: 120 credit points (8 units or modules).

The credit points for Year 3, the year abroad, are divided as follows:

- courses at foreign university: 30 credit points;
- dissertation (project): 30 points;
- profile: 60 points.

Profiling

The year abroad presents students with a new and exciting experience. However, the anticipation of this experience can cause anxiety to many students, particularly to those who have never been abroad except, perhaps, as tourists. Much is demanded of students once they are abroad: they have to get used to a new environment and to adapt to new and complex structures in a foreign society. They also have to become aware of cultural differences. This presents a real challenge which requires new insights. As a consequence, strategies and skills to cope with the new situation have to be developed. The profile offers students an opportunity to become aware of their learning in a foreign environment and helps them to reflect on this process.

Before they go abroad students are provided with a folder which contains a logbook and a form for the Record of Achievement. Students are required to keep a record of their progress in the logbooks, which have a list of transferable skills and qualities as headings. These are divided into five broad categories:

1. Organisation and initiative
   a) organise living environment: accommodation, health insurance, residence permit, bank, transport;
   b) organise academic programme: language course, other courses;
   c) organise research project: arrange appointments, interviews, material.
2. Communication
   a) use of academic/everyday/colloquial language/social interaction: socialising, shopping, discussions with tutors;
   b) listening: academic, TV/radio, accents, dialects;
   c) writing: academic (essay/project/coursework), administrative (filling in forms);
   d) reading: academic, media.
3. Personal and interpersonal
   a) working and relating;
   b) self-confidence;
   c) flexibility.
4. Cultural awareness
   a) reflecting on experience of the new culture;
   b) tolerance of different practices;
   c) participating in local communal activities.
5. Intellectual
   a) developing learning strategies;
   b) developing research strategies;
   c) problem solving.

Preparation

The specific placement most suitable for each student is usually decided in the second term of the second year, and students are briefed about their placement and the project they have to undertake. In the third term special sessions take place to prepare students for profiling.

In preparation for coming into contact with the different culture, students, for instance, discuss ways of identifying features of their own culture: social structures, lifestyle, national or physical characteristics. Students discuss how they perceive the foreign culture and further develop an awareness of cultural relativities, building on information they have previously received in class.

In these preparatory sessions students are given sample profiles with entries written by former students. The two components of the profile are the logbook and the Record of Achievement. Students are also given a checklist of skills and qualities, and after discussion they identify which skills they feel they need to develop. Students assess the level of skill they already have and consider what level they might realistically achieve. They are also encouraged to think of strategies to improve these skills as we shall later illustrate with an example.

These profiling preparation sessions provide a sound base for the students to develop skills in three ways. First, the fact that students themselves choose the skills which they want to improve places the responsibility for the year abroad on the students. Secondly, pinpointing these skills gives students a clearer view of what they want to achieve and finally, the strategies students consider will help them later on.

The Logbook

The logbook is a private record for the students and should be seen as aiding a process of constant reflection and self-analysis, highlighting both positive and negative feelings about the new experience. It is recommended that students write under the different entries once a month. A student who has difficulties in organising everyday life in Britain, for instance, might feel particularly anxious about organising enrolment and an academic programme in the foreign university or with practical concerns such as finding accommodation. This student might include organisational skills as an area for development and would be encouraged during the preparation sessions to think of strategies for improving. In the case of organisational skills this might involve keeping a diary, making lists etc. This student's entry in the logbook under Organisation and initiative for November might read as follows:

It seems I've had to organise so many things this month. It has never been my strongest point but I have learned the value of making lists. Also I have really had to use my initiative to find out how the system works at university, how to sign up for classes, find accommodation, work out how to get from home to college, where to shop etc. I felt so overwhelmed by it all but I used my lists to help me prioritise and tried to take things step by step. At least now I have done it all without too many problems.

By keeping a logbook students are forced to reflect regularly on the aims they have set themselves. This focuses them and helps the development of their skills. At the end of the year abroad students will look through their logbook and assess their progress in the various skills and qualities and transfer the information to the Record of Achievement.

The Record of Achievement

The Record of Achievement has the same headings but, unlike the logbook, which is a private record, it is a formal statement of the students' view of their development during their year abroad, supported by comments from the year abroad tutor. This document can be presented in the future to prospective employers together with job applications. As students will have the information about their skills and transferable qualities on record, and will have been made to give them a great deal of thought, they should be able to use this positively in the process of employment interviews.

The entry for Organisation and initiative in the Record of Achievement for the student considered above might read something like the following:

It was essential to have good organisational skills during my year abroad because the lecture schedule was very full and I had less time for personal study. I also worked part time teaching English. In my first month I had to choose my courses, find accommodation and familiarise myself with a different culture. I planned my time carefully to achieve a successful balance between work, study and leisure activities and had a very successful year. I have gained confidence in my ability to use my initiative and organisational skills to deal effectively with new situations.

We believe that the awareness of the learning process will be invaluable when the students start to look for employment at the end of their course, giving them a greater sense of their suitability in terms of a future career.

Employment

By engaging students in a reflective process about their own personal career and development plans it is our intention to encourage them to see themselves as employable. Humanities students in particular do not often see a direct correlation between their studies and their employability. Our aim is for our students to perceive and value themselves not exclusively as narrow, subject-based graduates of a particular discipline but, additionally, as possessing other skills, and hence to consider themselves suitable for a wide range of careers. Every year several of our graduates return to the country where they spent their year abroad to find employment with national and international companies or to do a further degree. Apart from the language skills and academic knowledge, the personal qualities and competences they acquired no doubt contribute to their employability. Informal talks with employers confirm that they value highly the personal qualities such as self-confidence, independence, flexibility and adaptability which the students acquire during the year abroad.

Conclusion

We believe that profiling the year abroad offers the following benefits.

1. It helps to formalise and assess the important non-academic learning which takes place during the year abroad.
2. It helps students identify the skills and personal qualities which they feel they need to develop.
3. By making the students reflect regularly on their progress, it helps them focus on the aims they have set themselves, thereby aiding the development of these skills.
4. It encourages students to take responsibility for their own learning during the year abroad both inside and outside the academic process.

Acknowledgements

Our thanks to Morag Anderson who prepared the students embarking on the year abroad for profiling and to Mary Noonan and Dave Edye who worked with us at the beginning of the project.

Chapter 11

Profiling in Chemistry Courses
Barbara A Page

Introduction

Most of the graduates from the School of Applied Chemistry progress into research and taught Masters courses. For some students this has been a positive choice but others have sought refuge in further study rather than face the arduous task of seeking employment. Over the past few years the School of Applied Chemistry has become increasingly concerned that many students do not enter work immediately on graduation and have considered methods for providing opportunities to enhance their prospects of gaining employment. The expectation of better job prospects is one of the main reasons why our students, most of whom are non-traditional entrants, come into higher education, but several factors had led to study programmes giving gradually a lower priority to the active development of more general, work-related, transferable skills.

One of the reasons why so many of our graduates proceed into research relates to the history and past experience of the school. Degree-level teaching in chemistry began in the late nineteenth century at what was then the Northern Polytechnic and students, in common with those from some of the other original polytechnics, studied for internal degrees from the University of London. The school's long history of degree study and consequent active commitment to research has led our graduates to believe that they should progress mostly into this area. The emphasis

106

placed correctly by the school on a thorough grounding in theoretical and practical chemistry had led, to a certain extent, to the interpretation that subject-specific expertise was of overwhelmingly greater importance than the improvement of generic skills. Students absorbed the view that they were being prepared primarily for a life in research and concentrated on achieving good results in their subject area, perceiving the development of more general skills as peripheral to the main aim of the courses. In the current highly competitive job market it is obviously critical that they appreciate the importance of possessing these fundamental skills and take steps to develop them.

Factors which have led to a reduction in the opportunities available for the development of employment-related skills have included changes in the length of the teaching year and the resulting syllabus pressures, and decreased staff to student ratios.

The Faculty of Science, Computing and Engineering has operated a modular scheme since 1973 and became part of the university-wide scheme when it was introduced in 1991/2. The institutional scheme brought with it a reduced teaching year and increased student choice of topics studied, both of which gave less time for the study of chemistry. This contraction in time available led to syllabus pressures arising as the knowledge-base in chemistry has proved difficult to reduce substantially. The extensive base is due to the requirements established and overseen by the professional accrediting institution, the need for comparability with European qualifications, and also because industry and academia demand well-informed and knowledgeable chemistry graduates.

Students studying science and engineering are relatively highly timetabled because of the necessity for laboratory and workshop practical work. Time needs to be spent gaining a 'feel' for the subject and acquiring essential manipulative techniques and practical skills. While there have been vigorous attempts to reduce the time spent on practical work it is thought that, in most courses, the limit has probably been reached. Employer comments about 'graduates lacking basic practical skills' are beginning to be heard and, after all, few of us would be happy to be operated on by a surgeon who had gained her/his skills from open-learning packs and paper exercises – important though these may be.

Finally, students in science and engineering tend to expect to be passive receivers of information and do not usually demand active participation in the teaching and learning process. In part this passivity results from the enormous knowledge-base, the reasons for which are explained above, and in part is due to the workloads usually associated with science and engineering subjects. The timetable, workload and the increasing necessity for students to work part time to finance their studies mean that they simply do not have large amounts of additional time to spend on other activities.

Thus we were seeking an effective and resource-efficient method, requiring a minimum of students' time, to help them become more aware of the transferable skills they should develop and how these might be strengthened within their subject studies and through external interests and activities. It was decided that some system of profiling their experiences was needed to enable students to identify their skills and to produce strategies for their improvement. The Profiling and Portfolio production project was initiated to meet this need.

The project

As stated above, the major aim of the project was to improve the employment prospects of students taking courses in chemistry by helping them to identify their general skills and to enable them to consider how these skills might be improved. In parallel with this was the hope that the project would encourage students to reflect on and plan their degree work, rather than just 'living though' their programme of study. Other aims of the project were to develop a suitable induction programme for new students and to lay the foundations for a three-year programme introducing profiling throughout the degree courses offered by the school, ie to have one entire cohort of students possessing a comprehensive profile on the development of their personal skills.

The project was based around a student Profiling and Portfolio pack (see Figure 11.1) developed during the summer vacation by staff from the school. It was focused only on year one degree students taking either single subject chemistry degrees or courses in which chemistry is a major component, as these form a fairly readily identifiable group within the modular scheme. Employers were invited to participate in the project and to comment on the pack contents and the skills targeted.

The pack contains sections on a variety of topics concerned with skills that are of relevance to both students' academic studies and to their future employment. Those deemed to be of especial importance to scientists are: numeracy; IT skills; communications – oral, written, presentational and graphical, listening; problem solving and analytical skills; practical skills; self-organisational and team-working skills. The skills selected broadly follow the essential, core skills identified by the National Council for Vocational Qualifications (NCVQ).

Each section contains questionnaires, planning grids and so on, and offers guidance on the effective use of the contents. The pack helps students to compile their personal record details and chronicle their skills development throughout the course. The portfolio section aids students in collecting and collating evidence demonstrating their possession of the selected skills; the evidence may be pieces of coursework, descriptions of activities, letters of commendation and results transcripts and certificates.

Introduction

Tasks summary	Indicates the sections/activities students should expect to complete and the time scale for their completion.
Summary CV	Sections for students to record their past history – qualifications, employment, interests and activities.
Course record	Provides an opportunity to record comprehensive details of the course of study – teaching and assignment timetables, modules taken, grades achieved, lecturing staff and overall performance (score card) on the degree.
Study skills	Gives guidance on effective study and covers, inter alia, note taking, using reference material, organisation of time, revision techniques, essay and report writing.
Transferable skills	This section looks at the selected skills and allows students to reflect on what they can do, where the skills is gained and how it can be improved. Free sheets are provided so that students can include individual, personal skills which they believe they possess or wish to develop.
Self-assessment	A questionnaire guides students towards greater self-awareness of their strengths and weaknesses and provides information about employment-related skills.
Careers	Contains timetables on the workshops and other sessions organised by the Careers Advisory Service for the School during the academic year.

Figure 11.1 *Profiling and Portfolio pack contents.*

Students were guided through the pack in workshop sessions held during the year.

The workshops

Three optional workshops were organised during the year and more than 80 per cent of the targeted students attended at least two of these. Typical workshop sessions involved two to four staff from the school and others, for example the faculty Enterprise in Higher Education coordinator and staff from the Careers Advisory Service, and were for 30–35 students. In addition to the workshops, a careers afternoon, with contributions from employers, was held during the year.

During the first two sessions students worked either individually, or more usually in groups, and covered topics such as study skills, personal evaluation, employers' requirements and transferable skills. The third session was used to evaluate the project and pack contents and to determine students' wishes with respect to activities in future workshops.

The first session, held during induction week, was used to introduce the packs and to provide guidance on study skills, self-organisation and time management. The importance of profiling their skills was discussed and students were taken slowly through the pack contents. It was thought appropriate that a relatively short, initial period should be devoted specifically to profiling as students might be intimidated by the sheer size of the pack and the quantity of information required. By the end of the workshop they had begun to complete the factual sections of the pack relating to their entry qualifications, interests and their course of study.

Two further, longer, structured sessions were arranged during the year – one in each semester. In the first session students were presented with a selection of advertisements relating to their subject specialism and required to develop an outline job specification for each position. Having analysed the posts they identified the common, general skills sought by employers and were encouraged to consider how they might develop these, both within their course and from external interests and everyday activities. After this students divided into groups and each group selected a particular general skill on which to work. Towards the end of the session a nominated spokesperson gave an informal five-minute summary of the group's discussions to the rest of the meeting.

The final workshop enabled students to reflect on the development and progress of their skills and was used to evaluate the project and the pack.

To supplement and reinforce the workshop sessions and provide continuity to the profiling process, individual student progress was monitored periodically throughout the year by the staff involved and recorded, by staff signature in the student's pack, and dated.

Students' views

Many useful and constructive comments were obtained from the students during the evaluation session. For example, they thought that some of the pack sections were too complicated and lengthy and that the individual up-dating sessions were too time consuming. They decided that the presentation of some sections could be improved and shortened (and gave ideas on these aspects) and that the amount of writing required should be reduced considerably. Students would have welcomed more workshop discussion sessions so that some of the ideas presented and skills explored could have been extended. They thought that the self-analysis section should, if wished, be a private document.

They agreed that they had gained some very positive benefits from using the pack and attending the workshops. The activities had helped them attain a greater understanding of the necessity of good study skills and had helped them to identify their skills – both academic and general. The project had made them start to think about what they needed to acquire for employment and had aided career planning. It had also given them confidence in organising their time and working with others. The session during induction week had been particularly welcomed as providing an informal introduction to other students and academic staff – giving a sense of 'belonging to a group' – and made them more confident in approaching their personal tutors and other staff during the initial stages of their course. Although all the students involved were studying Chemistry as a major part of their course, under the modular scheme students often have quite individual programmes of study and the workshop sessions were seen as an enjoyable method for the interchange of ideas and views on their personal development and study programmes in general.

At the end of the year students believed that the project had made them more conscious of their skills and abilities and had helped them to cope better with the demands of their studies.

Employers' views

Employers were consulted both by informal discussion and through more formal sessions and a number of helpful views were given. In general, they approved the aims of the project and agreed they were seeking the skills on which the project focused. Chemistry graduates are selected both on their subject-specific knowledge, understanding and abilities, and on generic skills. Employers are seeking recruits who have developed these skills from a range of activities, internal and external to their academic study, and are interested particularly in the demonstration of communications and group-working skills. It was essential that students were made aware of the importance of acquiring these skills as they proceeded through their degree. Employers are selecting graduates with management potential and while the average chemist might begin her/his career at the bench, career patterns often meant a gradual move away from the laboratory into other activities, for which more general skills would be vital.

Additionally, many employers are starting to introduce systems for recording staff achievement and career development and these are similar to the process under trial in chemistry. Giving students the ideas and tools of self-development and career planning at an early stage thus provides a useful introduction to the procedures they will meet in employment.

While employers could not envisage profiles being used in the selection procedure – it would be just too time consuming – it was thought that the document should allow students to complete application forms more readily and improve their self-presentational skills, both of which skills are often woefully absent in many science graduates.

However, a cautionary note was offered. They were very concerned that students should not lose sight of the subject requirements of work in industry – industry needs employees to have a sound, substantial subject-knowledge base and understanding and to have acquired well-developed practical skills. Although transferable skills are important, employers were emphatic that the development of these should not be at the expense of a reduced background in chemistry.

The future

The second phase of the project was begun during the 1994/5 session and has included the provision of a revised pack to new, year one students, amended along the lines suggested by the trial group. A programme of activities has been devised to ensure the continuing interest of year two students and these will concentrate more specifically on employment-gaining skills. For example, sessions are being held on exploring students' values and interests, helping them to produce a CV and complete application forms and developing their performance in interviews. These sessions are organised with the Careers Advisory Service and have the involvement of employers and academic staff. The project will be fully evaluated when a complete cohort of students graduate but, so far, the project has met with approval from the students and has led to a greater involvement of employers with the School of Applied Chemistry. Finally, it has encouraged staff to identify where they might provide opportunities for the development of generic, employment-related skills within the chemistry courses.

Chapter 12

Profiling in an Integrated BA Business Studies Programme

Anne Brockbank

Introduction

The university's commitment to personal competence profiling was implemented in the Business School through projects seeking to develop profiling approaches for particular courses. The projects focused on profile packages with the objective of *enabling students to articulate and communicate what they can do, using the language of transferable skills.* Profiling projects would seek to help students to recognise and assess the skills they possess or have gained or enhanced, and to be able to demonstrate these to prospective employers. Ideally the process would begin at the start of a programme of study, carry on throughout the programme and culminate at the point of employment, on graduation.

This chapter describes one Business School project: the development, implementation and evaluation of a profile structure designed to complement a module of the COMBUS degree. COMBUS (the BA Combined Studies in Business) is a new scheme, started in 1993, whereby students undertake studies in two pathways (known as half-degrees), combining subjects like business law, marketing, international business, economics and employment studies.

	Preliminary Level	Intermediate Level	Final Level
International Business (IB)	Introduction to Economics Principles of Marketing	International Marketing (M) International Procurement and Operations	Issues in International Business International Business in the Far East
	Introduction to Finance Economics and Political History	International Business Economics Economics and Politics in Europe	International Business in Europe Cross-Cultural Management
Law in Business (BL)	Law in Business Business Skills	Law of Business Organisations Consumer Protection Law	Current Issues in Law International Law
	Common Law Liabilities in Business EC Law	International Law of Contracts Employment Law	Industrial Relations Law Competition Law

Figure 12.1 *Specimen programme for BA (Hons) International Business and Law in Business.*

The proposed profiling system was to be integrated with the core (compulsory) module Business Skills so that all students taking the scheme would be given the opportunity to experience profiling. The Business Skills workshop, a core module, is compulsory for all first-year, or preliminary level, students. The positioning of the Business Skills module in a sample programme can be seen in Figure 12.1.

The COMBUS degree scheme aims to 'provide students with opportunities for the acquisition of and development of transferable technical, study, social and interpersonal skills and competences which will be of value to their personal development in their careers and beyond' (DD, 1993). One such opportunity is offered by the Business Skills (core) module, which 'is designed to provide students with the opportunity to develop a wide range of generic skills' and 'to assist students in the development of their independent learning skills'.

In particular the module would form a base for the introduction of an integrated profiling system. Students would be offered the opportunity to work on their personal competence profile alongside their attendance and completion of the Business Skills module. The module would provide input relating to the development areas covered by the profile, and module tutors would guide students through the profile itself.

Our approach

The development team of four were academic staff of considerable experience in the development of skills in adults. One of the team, Jan Bamford, was also acting as COMBUS course tutor and was therefore very familiar with the philosophy of the scheme as well as its complicated structure. The team benefited from Miriam Green who, as a longstanding member of the Business School staff, has varied and extensive experience of skills development for undergraduates and student-centred 'skills' programmes. The third member of the team, Barbara Reik, came from a training and development background, with high-level experience as a trainer in industry. The remaining member of the team, myself, while an academic of some years experience, was also familiar with experiential training methods in the world of work.

In order to integrate the profile with the Business Skills module the team started with the module programme, deciding what sessions we could offer in order to meet the module requirements laid down in the syllabus. The aims of the module include development of intrapersonal, interpersonal and group *awareness* in students; an *understanding* of communication and process in particular modes of discourse; as well as a *realisation* that learning has (hopefully) occurred. Given the very limited time resources allocated to the module, these aims were somewhat ambitious and curriculum evolution has ensured that the module now attracts additional time resources.

The Business Skills workshop

The team struggled to provide sessions which would meet the aims of the module with the limited contact time of 22.5 hours, as computing skills were allocated half of the available 45 hours. The qualities of the team are reflected in the creative design of the module, using the same session to address a variety of objectives. The team decided to experiment with three-hour sessions, rather than the usual one and a half, so that skills sessions occurred every fortnight, alternating with computing. The three-hour sessions were designed to allow time for students to reflect on their learning, understand how and if they had learned, as well as give some attention to their profile. The impact of this innovation will be discussed below. Students were allocated a skills tutor for the module in groups of 17 and the four tutors involved in creating the profile portfolio were also the module tutors.

Our approach to the module was to offer students a choice of methods of communication, in the sense of modes of discourse, as well as the nuts and bolts of transmitting and receiving messages. The programme deliberately set out to challenge the dualism of traditional and academic styles of communication as oppositional and unproductive, particularly where the goal is consensus. The three modes covered by the programme are

- adversarial, with academic and UK legal applications;
- inquisitorial, with its European legal and problem-solving applications;
- consensual, with its European, international and corporate applications.

The notion of alerting students at the outset to the normative arrangements of academic and business communities equips them to question and reflect on the power structures which maintain these arrangements in place, as givens, if not challenged. The importance of discourse as the vehicle for socially constructed meaning and the ideology of language is emphasised in the programme by the use of cooperative rather than hierarchical facilitation methods. Traditional models of teaching and learning, where tutors hold the balance of power, in hierarchical mode, maintains that power and limits analysis of it. Cooperative methods, on the other hand, offer students the possibility of sharing power, and, if properly structured, encourage analysis of power structures within the learning group. See Heron (1993) for a detailed discussion of facilitation methods.

As much of the material used by students was generated by themselves, this gave opportunities to highlight power structures such as gender and class, embedded within the learning group. Students were invited to experience the three modes of discourse described above, discuss their relative merits, and assess their usefulness in particular situations. The skills needed for effective performance in each mode relate to the 11 skill areas covered in the profile, described below.

Preparing the profile

The team worked in pairs, with two creating a draft, submitting it to the other two for comments, and redesigning on the basis of feedback. What emerged was a package of material in an A4 ring binder in 11 sections preceded by an introduction. (See pages 125–31 for selected sections from the package.)

The 11 sections covered skill areas as follows.

1. Personal skills: awareness of self, confidence, self-discipline and self-care.
2. Assertiveness skills: approaching others, standing up for oneself, agreeing/disagreeing, making requests and taking risks.
3. Communication skills: oral, graphic and written channels, researching, analysing and organising.
4. Interpersonal skills: listening, observing, disclosing and reflecting.
5. Problem-solving skills: defining, critical thinking, creativity and innovation.
6. Group skills: forming, team working, organising and following through.
7. Computing skills: keyboard, wordprocessing, database and spreadsheets.
8. Evaluation skills: clarifying and reflecting, personal learning.
9. Emotional skills: identifying, expressing and responding to others.
10. Negotiation skills: persuading, responding and negotiating an outcome.
11. Feedback skills: giving and receiving feedback.

Each section consisted of:

- a skills survey with rating scale
- a self-assessment document
- a peer-assessment document
- a tutor-assessment document.

Each skill survey (self-administered) consists of a bank of statements to be rated by the student on a five-point scale as follows:

- 1 = I would like to acquire this skill
- 2 = I would like to brush up on this skill
- 3 = I can do this sometimes
- 4 = I can do this quite well
- 5 = I can do this very well.

After completion of the skill survey students would attend a workshop session designed to develop, practise or enhance the skill in question. Workshop material enables students to develop their skills in the session itself with tutor and colleagues, or afterwards, for example, by practising assertive behaviour in social situations.

Self-assessment, peer-assessment and tutor-assessment documents follow a similar format, asking for examples of the student's use of the skill in question; *how, when* and *where*. It is insufficient for the student to describe and discuss the skill. The student must present *an instance* of its use and the context and outcome. Where tutors have observed such instances in the workshop session they may complete the tutor-assessment sheet. Documents are to be signed by the student/peer/tutor as appropriate. Examples of skill surveys and assessment documents appear at the end of this chapter.

In designing the profile Reik and I decided to follow a formative design, in three stages: self-assessment, practice and evidence. First students rate themselves against learning outcomes (skills) described in behavioural terms in the profile, using the five-point rating scale described above. The workshop session provides input and practice in relation to the skill in question and students are encouraged to seek opportunities outside the workshop to practise and improve their skill. For instance, presentation skills may be developed in other modules and critical feedback provided by other tutors. After working on and/or practising the skill or competence in question students provide evidence of their acquisition or enhancement of it, from themselves (self-assessment), their peers (peer assessment) and their tutors (tutor assessment). These assessment documents encourage students to cite *examples* of their use or deployment of particular skills. Where appropriate, students may re-rate themselves against the original learning outcomes to show an improved rating.

The presentation of evidence of development from self and others provides valuable material within such a formative document. The profile may be used as a basis for a summative document at the end of a student's course of study, providing a Record of Achievement or a tutor's reference.

The preparation of the portfolio was a long process of sifting and editing materials from other sources, including other profile packs used in the university. Materials from other training programmes, if appropriate, were altered to suit and, where necessary, new material was created. Reik and I sought to cover the three domains of Bloom's taxonomy of educational objectives (Bloom, 1964) so that physical, intellectual and emotional behaviour was described in the 11 profile sections outlined above.

Bamford and Green offered advice and comments at intervals and the profile emerged in time for the first ever cohort of the COMBUS degree which enrolled in September 1993.

Introducing the profile to students

The profile pack included a cover sheet, personal details, a table of contents and an introduction. The introduction, written in plain English, emphasises that the profile is for the student's benefit, that it will operate alongside the Business Skills workshop and that it will not be assessed. In addition the purpose of the profile in terms of providing evidence for future employers is explained, and a description of the profile with a section on how to complete the documents is included.

The induction session at the beginning of the workshop included time for students to understand and discuss with tutors the purpose of the profile and how to complete it. For many students the approach was completely novel and they needed time to get used to it. Tutors found that clarification was asked for throughout the semester, with some skill areas being more problematic than others. For example, students were unsure about how to record instances of their use of interpersonal skills such as listening and disclosure, or their group skills. Tutors were able to help them to use the tutorial group as a source of feedback on behaviour.

The integration of the profile with the workshop programme can be seen in the parallel programmes below.

Approximately 60 per cent of the areas of development covered in the profile portfolio were addressed in module sessions. The portfolio was designed to cover development over the period of study, in the case of COMBUS, three academic years. Although there is no further direct provision for skills development in the degree programme, students may be given opportunities to develop in the remaining 40 per cent of the areas covered in the portfolio.

Evaluation of the profile

It proved nearly impossible for students to evaluate the profile separately from the skills workshop itself. However, a comprehensive and thorough evaluation programme was carried out, comprising student question-naires, group discussions, tutor questionnaires and employer interviews. The report based on this evaluation programme has been described as a fine model of evaluation procedures and a possible model for future evaluations (EHE, 1994). Nevertheless, the difficulty of unravelling the perceptions of students relating to a programme of work from the profiling process itself may need to be addressed where integration is desired.

The evaluation process

The profile is intended to be used by students at the start of their studies, throughout their period of study and, as graduands/graduates, at the point of seeking employment. Therefore students' perceptions of its relevance for their studies, its accessibility and ease of use, as well as perceived benefits for the future, were evaluated. Employers/graduate recruiters evaluated the profile on similar criteria, and tutors were also asked to evaluate the package.

Sessions	Profile plan
Induction: All students	Contents page
'How we will work'	Personal details
Approach to learning	Introduction
	Philosophy
Explanation of project	Section description
Seminar groups	Section plan
Ice-breaker	Explanation
Personal tutorial arrangements	
Language test	
Exercise: What I do well	
Tutor's notes	
1. Exercises in small groups	Section 1
(ideally personal tutorial groups)	Skills survey 1
Good/bad learning experiences	
Introduce package	
Lifeline	Lifeline
Life concepts	Life concepts
	Self-assessment 1
	Tutor assessment 1
	Peer assessment 1
2. Assertiveness workshop	Section 2
Plenary session and	Skills survey 2
exercises in small groups	Self-assessment 2
Rights	Tutor assessment 2
Dyads and triads	Peer assessment 2
Role-play material	
Assertion Q	
Model of assertion	
3. Presentations workshop	Section 3
Report writing	Skills survey 3
Essay writing	Self-assessment 3
Graphic communication	Tutor assessment 3
Oral presentations: individual	Peer assessment 3
Modes of discourse (1) debate	
4. Interpersonal skills	Section 4
Listening	Skills survey 4
Observing	Self-assessment 4
Reflecting	Tutor assessment 4
Disclosure	Peer assessment 4

Sessions	Profile plan

5. Problem exploration techniques
Lateral thinking
Brainstorming
Logic exercise
Exercise in reframing:
   Share research in twos
   Feedback in fours
Modes of discourse (2)
	Section 5
	Skills survey 5
	Self-assessment 5
	Peer assessment 5
	Tutor assessment 5

6. Group skills workshop Synergy and consensus Decision making Modes of discourse (3) Fish bowl exercise Assessment: group presentation	Section 6 Skills survey 6 Self-assessment 6 Tutor assessment 6 Peer assessments 6
7. Computing Sessions as arranged	Section 7 Skills survey 7 Self-assessment 7 Tutor assessment 7 Peer assessment 7
8. Evaluation of course Evaluation of profile pack Random selection for group discussion	Section 8 Evaluation document

End of module

Recommended further sessions

9. Recruitment and selection Interviewing Managing emotion; discipline and grievance, counselling Empathy workshop	Section 9 Skills survey 9 Self-assessment 9 Tutor assessment 9 Peer assessment 9
10. Negotiation skills Managing conflict Confrontation workshop	Section 10 Skills survey 10 Self-assessment 10 Tutor assessment 10 Peer assessment 10
11. Feedback workshop Challenge and development skills	Section 11 Skills survey 11 Self-assessment 11 Tutor assessment 11 Peer assessment 11

Figure 12.2 *COMBUS Business Skills workshop programme.*

The criteria to be evaluated were as follows:

- ease of completion
- relevance
- benefit to candidate in the future
- effectiveness
- general impression of the portfolio
- omitted material.

Students evaluated the profile through feedback forms provided in the portfolio, structured questionnaires and group discussions with tutors. Tutors evaluated the profile through similar forms and questionnaires as well as a formal review session at the end of the semester. Two representatives of prospective future employers were interviewed using a schedule based on the student and tutor evaluation documents. The interviews were carried out informally by two members of the profile team.

Results

Students were generally positive about the profile, but a small minority were thoroughly upset by it. For some the significance of their behaviour and the importance of transferable skills is not a high priority, and this was revealed in comments like 'employers will not want it' and 'it was too personal'.

Mature students were strongly supportive of the profile, seeing it as 'relevant' and 'useful', perhaps because they had already been employed and knew the value of such a document to employers. Many students confirmed that the profile and/or the module programme had caused them to 'think seriously' about their behaviour and personal skills, and its function in enabling them to 'evaluate the skills required for business' and 'think about how good or bad I am at certain skills' was mentioned by nearly all the students. There was strong support for the benefits of the profile (or did they mean the workshop?) in developing their 'group skills' and 'communication skills'.

The need to provide a concrete example from their real life had defeated many of them, a consequence perhaps of the emphasis in secondary and tertiary education on abstraction to the exclusion of practice (Hemming, 1980). The profile was demanding a completely new and unfamiliar approach to self- and other-analysis, requiring evidence of *observed behaviour* rather than discussion around the skill concerned. A minority of students found the emotional skills surveys and assessment documents disturbing, seeing the area as primarily negative (there were no examples of joy or pleasure in assessment documents) and therefore a potential threat if revealed to employers.

The prospect of presenting the complete profile to an employer was not relished by students, and they complained about carrying the A4 file around with them. However, there was no doubt that the ringbinder form of the profile was awkward and that completion of the assessment documents had been difficult for students.

All tutors believed that the profile would be beneficial to students in the future, but agreed that it was difficult for them to complete. Tutors confirmed that the size of the package was a problem, and that the assessment documents had presented difficulties to tutors and students at such an early stage in the programme, where relationships had not properly developed. The three-hour sessions had definite advantages, giving space for reflection on the learning process, but students and tutors were unhappy about lack of contact in the intervening week. Recognition of the importance of regular contact in modular schemes has ensured that future programmes will provide for weekly contact with skills/personal tutors.

Both employer representatives confirmed that the portfolio, in its present form, is too big, certainly for presentation to a prospective employer. However, there was strong support for the A4 ringbinder as a *working document* for the student to draw on at the point of recruitment/ selection. Employers made positive comments about the layout of the portfolio; the behavioural definitions of each skill; the developmental approach; the demand for concrete evidence in assessment documents; written other-assessment and the emphasis throughout on student ownership of the process. The content of the profile was broadly in line with competences sought by our two employer contacts, except for the section on emotional skills, which is normally covered under personal strengths and human relations. Furthermore, employers say that they don't need tutor assessment. They are looking for the student's own claims, backed up by evidence and endorsed by their tutor. Both employer representatives were clear that the personal skills of candidates were of more interest to them than the class of degree.

Conclusion

Introduction of profile portfolios may be more appropriate at intermediate or final level, rather than right at the beginning of a programme of study when students are unfamiliar with the institution, tutors and each other. Skills development has traditionally been placed at preliminary level (following the remedial model) and we would question the necessity for this except where there are clear needs for operational skills like presentations, essays and reports. Students may benefit from a settling-in period, getting to know their peers and tutors, before feeling ready to analyse their behaviour and attitudes.

The portfolio is ambitious and students noted that the skills module only touched the surface of possible development for them. Many felt cheated by this and wondered when more would be provided. The allocated hours for skill development and portfolio work were insufficient. Students and staff want to meet once a week for three hours to establish good relationships and work on their development.

The layout of the portfolio, its size etc needs to be changed so that students can access it easily, without having to carry heavy files around. The revised profile is a more user-friendly package for everyday use, comprising an A5 Filofax-style student organiser and the A4 ringbinder for filing documents such as lecture notes, at home. Very little change is needed in the material content, apart from the section about emotional skills, always a no-go area in the business and academic world, which will need to be camouflaged inside other sections for use at preliminary level.

Resources for the Business Skills module in future programmes have been doubled, giving much-needed time for the processes described above. The curriculum is already evolving and developing with the experience of tutors and feedback from students. The module has been recognised by development teams as playing a key role in supporting students following a modular programme, where the reference group changes regularly, and the skills group remains a 'secure base' for students at the start of their studies in higher education.

There is evidence that an intermediate-level or final-level module would enable students to produce a more powerful bank of evidence for a future employer. For example, reports of student performance in simulated interviews, negotiations and conflict resolutions could provide material of the type being sought by future employers.

References

Bloom B (1956, 1964) *The Taxonomy of Educational Objectives*, Longman, London, Volumes 1 and 2.

Hemming J (1980) *The Betrayal of Youth: Secondary education must be changed*, M Boyars, London.

Heron J (1989) *The Facilitators' Handbook*, Kogan Page, London.

University of North London (1993) BA Combined Business Half Degree Scheme Definitive Document, University of North London, May.

Appendix

The following material is reproduced from selected section of the COMBUS Profiling Project 1993–4.

Combined Business Half Degree Scheme (COMBUS): Personal Profile

Name	
Course	
Period of study	
Course Tutor	
Year 1 Personal (Skills) Tutor	Room
Year 2 Personal Tutor	Room
Address	
Change of Address	

Note
This document contains confidential information. Please return it as soon as possible to the address above or to the University.

INTRODUCTION

This profile is for you. It is designed to take you through the personal skills needed for *getting on with people* as a student, as a graduate and ultimately as an employee.

Many of the skills in this profile you will have already. Some skills may be new to you and the *Business Skills workshop* module will provide you with opportunities to improve your personal skills as you desire.

Whether you have skills and want to enhance them, or would like to learn new skills, this profile is a record for your future. When you present yourself for placement and later, employment, it will provide evidence that you have the skills needed for working productively with others.

What exactly is a profile?
A profile is a document which records a student's development and/or skills acquired in the academic setting, in the workplace or elsewhere. Remember that a great deal of learning occurs outside the classroom and lecture theatre!

Why do we need profiles?
Evidence of personal transferable skills is provided by focusing on *what you can do* rather than *what you say you can do* and this evidence is being requested when you apply for placement and/or employment. More details of the project can be found on the next page.

PHILOSOPHY

The University of North London is committed to a programme of development for all students, which includes provision of a *profile*, in order to facilitate the learning process and provide evidence of your achievement of personal transferable skills.

The profile presented here is designed to enable you to recognise and assess the competences, qualities and skills you possess at the beginning of your course. Further, the profile will record your personal development throughout your studies at this university. When completed, your profile forms a portfolio of evidence about your personal skills, which you will be able to take with you after graduation.

The philosophy behind the project can be summarised as follows:

The University [sic] wants its graduates to be able to communicate and demonstrate more effectively the capacities of trained investigative minds, of high skill competences and of transferable academic and social skills in order that they can realise their potential more fully within their chosen spheres of activity. The process is conceived as one of interaction and interchange mutually beneficial to students, to employers and to the institution (EHE Proposal, April 1990).

Your contribution to the Enterprise project
This is a pilot programme. That means your experience of using it will help us to design the programme in its final version. So any difficulties you find in the package, or issues which give rise to confusion, are important for us to know about.

Please make a note of any such factors as you proceed through the profile package. Blank pages are provided at the end of each section for your use. Towards the end of the package you will find evaluation documents. We ask you to leave completion of these until the end of the workshop course, when a session has been allocated for the purpose.

The COMBUS Profile

The profile is laid out in 11 sections, the first six corresponding to your Business Skills workshop programme.

Each section offers the following:

1 A skills survey covering individual needs in the skill area in question. This is a self-assessment of your ability in one or two personal and interpersonal skills.
2 A brief description of a particular skill area. Additional material will be provided at each workshop.
3 Assessment documents which can be copied:
   Self
   Peer
   Tutor
   Other
4 Blank sheets for comments.

How to complete the skill surveys in each section
There are several skills people need to make use of almost every day in order to get along with other people and feel good about themselves. These skills are important.

We would like to know which skills you feel you have and which skills you would like to work on.

You will be asked to rate yourself for every skill. If you do not understand a word, or you are unsure about what a skill description means, please ask the person who gave you this survey.

There are no right or wrong answers; we are only interested in your own assessment of your skills. Please do not skip any items.

How to complete the assessments in each section
Three assessments are offered:

- self
- tutor
- peer.

Skills are itemised as they appear in the skills survey at the beginning of each section. It is your responsibility to complete assessments as and when you feel confident in that skill.

- *Self-assessment*. This *must* be completed fully. It is essential.
- *Tutor assessment*. This should be completed *where possible* (eg tutors may not see you demonstrate every skill).
- *Peer assessment*. This will be completed *where possible* (eg as group members may not see you demonstrate every skill).

Skills survey

Below you will find a list of skills. Read each skill carefully and rate yourself by putting a circle around the most appropriate number based on the following scale.

5 I can do this very well
4 I can do this quite well
3 I can do this sometimes
2 I would like to brush up on this skill
1 I would like to acquire this skill

Assertiveness skills

1	*Starting a conversation*: talking to someone about light topics.	1	2	3	4	5
2	*Carrying on a conversation*: opening the main topic and elaborating on it.	1	2	3	4	5
3	*Ending a conversation*: letting the other person know that you have been paying attention, and then closing the conversation appropriately.	1	2	3	4	5
4	*Making the first move in relationships*: as with a stranger at a party, nightclub, in college etc.	1	2	3	4	5
5	*Developing rapport*: taking time to converse with others.	1	2	3	4	5
6	*Standing up for yourself*: by letting other people know what you need, want, think or feel.	1	2	3	4	5

  7 *Agree/disagree*: being able to disagree (or agree)
     when you choose.   1 2 3 4 5
  8 *Saying yes/no*: being able to say no (or yes)
     when you choose.   1 2 3 4 5
  9 *Making requests*: requesting help in handling a
     difficult situation which you have not been
     able to manage by yourself.   1 2 3 4 5
 10 *Giving instructions*: clearly explaining to
     someone how you would like a specific task
     done.   1 2 3 4 5
 11 *Preparing for a stressful conversation*: planning
     ahead of time to present your point of view in
     a conversation which may be difficult.   1 2 3 4 5
 12 *Taking risks*: making a statement and sticking
     to it under pressure.   1 2 3 4 5
 13 *Apologising*: when appropriate telling someone
     sincerely that you are sorry for something you
     have done to cause them discomfort.   1 2 3 4 5

Self assessment
Assertiveness skills

Give an example of your use of each skill – how, when and where.

1 Starting a conversation:

2 Carrying on a conversation:

3 Ending a conversation:

4 Making the first move in relationships:

5 Developing rapport:

6 Standing up for yourself:

7 Agree/disagree:

8 Saying yes/no:

9 Making requests:

10 Giving instructions:

11 Preparing for a stressful conversation:

12 Taking risks:

13 Apologising:

Signature of student ....

Tutor assessment
Assertiveness skills

Give an example, where possible, of each student's use of each skill – how, when and where.

1 Starting a conversation:

2 Carrying on a conversation:

3 Ending a conversation:

etc.

Signature of tutor ....

Peer assessment
Assertiveness skills

Give an example, where possible, of student's use of each skill – how, when and where.

1   Starting a conversation:

2   Carrying on a conversation:

3   Ending a conversation:

etc.

Signature of group member ....

Section Three:

Curriculum Development and Transferable Skills

In addition to the profiling projects, described in the previous section, there have been a number of curriculum development projects at the University of North London which have set out to enhance or develop students' transferable skills. The following section provides a snapshot, covering a range of subject areas, of some of these projects.

Trevor Joscelyne describes the development of a module, within the English pathway of the Humanities modular scheme, on publishing. A large part of the teaching of the programme is conducted by professionals from the industry; and students then go out and spend a period of time on placement with book publishers, for example Virago or Bloomsbury, or with magazine publishers. Joscelyne describes the kinds of skill developed by students. Kathryn Castle presents a project in history designed to develop 'increased competence in written and oral expression'; and Susan Williamson describes a project on architecture, designed to facilitate the development of students' drawing abilities. Finally Nicole McBride and Karen Seago recount how they developed a Hypertext-based package to help students acquire grammatical skills in a number of languages.

Chapter 13

Getting into Print: An Introduction to the Publishing Industry

Trevor Joscelyne

This chapter recounts how, under the auspices of the Enterprise in Higher Education (EHE) initiative a module has been developed at the University of North London for students on the BA (Hons) English pathway within the Humanities modular scheme. It will seek to demonstrate how the module has been developed in response both to the changing definition of English studies and to the needs of a changing student profile. In this way the 'enterprise skills' and the employment awareness that the module (among other things) seeks to develop in students become an integral part of the curriculum and not an adjunct or polarity, posing a potential conflict of interest or blurring of focus for the students concerned.

The BA (Hons) English degree at North London has constantly evolved in response both to the changing nature of the discipline and to the needs of the student body. By the late 1980s degree-level English had already been taught at the university (formerly the Polytechnic of North London) for a quarter of a century. The teaching of English Studies there had originated in the external BA (Hons) of the University of London in the mid-1960s at a time when not even the development of the campus universities was catering for all the well-qualified A level applicants resulting from the postwar baby boom who wished to read for a degree in English. As is well known this situation led to the Robbins-inspired definition and expansion of higher education in the later 1960s, including the designation of the polytechnics. For the most part, however, the expansion at that point was catering primarily for increased numbers of the 18-year-old cohort and offering an essentially traditional degree programme. Certainly that was the initial picture with English Studies at North London in the mid to late 1960s.

Since then the curriculum of the degree, its mode of delivery and the body of students following the degree has undergone significant change at North London (as elsewhere). Throughout these developments, and to this day, the BA (Hons) English degree at North London has sought to combine the best of the traditional curriculum of English Studies with the best in innovative practice. It is within this context that the Introduction to the Publishing Industry can best be understood. By the late 1980s, both under the Council for National Academic Awards' auspices and more latterly after the university took responsibility for its own degree programmes, the English degree has come to be characterised by what might be termed 'contemporaneity': not just extensive provision for the study of contemporary literature, but more importantly the application of contemporary approaches and methodologies to the reading of all literature. Such contemporaneity had been stimulated not just by internal, national and international debates on the nature of the discipline – lively as these had been in the 1970s and early 1980s – but also by the interests and needs of students.

By the late 1980s the University of North London had established a national reputation for facilitating access to higher education and for providing higher education for the whole community. The English programmes of study had played a significant role within the humanities in advancing and realising the university's mission of increased access. By the late 1980s also the profile of English students at North London had become *predominantly* mature, *predominantly* female, and multiracial. In being *predominantly* mature it was also *predominantly* local and hence reflected the innercity and metropolitan nature of the institution. Developments within the content of the curriculum, such as the emphasis on contemporary literature, on women's writing and on new (post-colonial) literatures in English, all reflected the social and intellectual interests and needs of such students. So, too, did the underpinning of many of the approaches to the reading of literature, such as feminism, structuralism and deconstruction.

While the intellectual needs of a radically different body of students had been catered for by on-course developments, what had not been addressed to the same extent was the needs that these students (and similar students on other programmes) might have with regard to employment and other opportunities after completion of their degrees. Consequently the major impetus in the university's bid to the Employment Department to be included in the EHE initiative was a desire to carry forward the access mission from the point of entry to the point of delivery and to the point of exit. The university's access misssion was not thought to be complete unless equality of access to higher education was carried through to equality of career opportunity and it was recognised that this had implications for the nature of the curriculum, its mode of delivery and its assessment. The university was successful in being included in the fourth round of EHE and the university's EHE programme began in September 1991.

The key features of the university's proposed programme were the development of systems of student profiling (or Records of Achievement) and the simultaneous development of curriculum or learning development projects, related to competence-based or work-related learning, which would enhance the profile of student capabilities. With respect to this programme, the profile of the English students at North London posed challenges from three particular perspectives. First, English and humanities graduates enter a very wide range of occupations on graduation, many of which do not draw directly on the content of the curriculum they have followed. Secondly, their maturity, gender balance, predominant class background and cultural diversity meant that they did not conform to the stereotype many employers still have of a graduate, namely a white middle-class 22–25-year-old. Thirdly, because of their maturity, the majority have some form of work experience, in many cases extensive and in some cases at a very responsible level. Consequently generic work experience in and of itself was not a means of providing the confidence and specific knowledge and experience to facilitate access to satisfying and potentially influential positions within chosen areas of employment.

Since the initial process of bidding to the Training, Enterprise and Education Directorate (TEED) began two years before the programme was established, it had been possible to undertake some preparatory work, and this was especially true of the publishing module. By 1988 the English degree programmes had been located in course structure terms within a humanities modular degree scheme and in resource and academic development terms within the School of Literary and Media Studies. The school had brought together work in the cognate disciplines of literature and media, notably Film and Theatre Studies, and had a common theoretical base in signifying practices. This convergence of cognate disciplines focused greater interest in the material production of literature, a feature not very pronounced in most traditional literature curricula, in alignment to interests in forms of media production. A sector of employment in which many students of literature and media think they would like to work is publishing and the media industries. This sector is also perceived to be difficult to access because of its popularity and 'glamour'. It was therefore felt to be a relevant and challenging field in which to start and one in which work-related learning could be related and integrated to mainstream issues in the degree programme of English students, since the value of the unit was never conceived as narrowly or purely vocational. For example, the unit was also conceived to enable students to have a better understanding of such issues as the relationship between 'value' defined in economic or market terms and 'value' in literary, aesthetic or cultural terms. Such issues can only be seriously addressed when students are able to combine insights from people and experience in the industry with theoretical reflection and analysis.

Prior, therefore, to the start of the EHE programme, the school commissioned a freelance editor working in the publishing industry to undertake a feasibility study with a limited number of publishers in both the book and magazine sectors to see whether publishers perceived value in the provision of work-related learning with regard to the publishing industry, and whether and how they would cooperate in the provision of short-term placements and other contributions to the programme. The response from publishers in both the book and magazine sectors was sufficiently encouraging for the school to develop an optional module within the degree pathway and to have it validated through the quality assurance mechanisms of the university so that it was ready to run as a fully assessed, credit-bearing unit in the first year of the EHE programme, 1991–2. In fact, the school had validated a module template, Introduction to the Media Industries, within which introductions to specific media industries, such as publishing, could be developed and validated.

The module was conceived and developed primarily by Claire Buck, Trevor Griffiths and myself in the role I then held as Head of School. The unit was coordinated and delivered essentially by Claire Buck, for whose help I am grateful in documenting this development. It comprises a 15-week module, (including assessment time), which has normally been delivered in the second semester in order to accommodate a three-week placement around the Easter vacation period, although it has been delivered in the first semester with the work placement prepared for during the preceding academic year and taking place in the summer vacation prior to formal delivery of the unit.

In the standard form of delivery, in the pre-placement period five key issues of publishing are addressed:

1. the nature of the publishing industry: the different forms of publishing and the relationships between the trades and professions which constitute it;
2. the making of a book or magazine: the stages and processes of the material production of the book or magazine;
3. issues of editorial policy and the constraints within which this operates, such as legal and financial frameworks;
4. marketing and promotion of books and magazines (which has proved remarkably interesting to and popular with student participants);
5. the contribution and potential of new technologies within the publishing industry.

English students at North London are particularly well placed to appreciate the last topic, since a distinctive feature of all the pathways within the Humanities modular scheme is that a unit in information technology is compulsory at the preliminary level. Many students take optional units in information technology at advanced level, such as desktop publishing. Students can then combine this interest in IT with other dimensions of English studies such as creative writing or the publishing unit under consideration.

Formal inputs into study of all the above topics is made by professionals from the industry, either personnel from companies which offered placements or from people working freelance in the industry. Approximately 60 per cent of the teaching contact is delivered by personnel from the industry. In all, 18 publishing companies have participated in delivery of the unit, either through the provision of placements or inputs into teaching. There were up to ten students on the unit. The companies have ranged from large companies which are household names in book or magazine publishing (such as Bloomsbury, Virago and Ideal Home), through specialist companies (such as Kogan Page, Harcourt Brace Jovanovitch and Stonehart Leisure Magazines), to publishers with a community interest (like Greenpeace and X Books) and in-house publications like the university's own internal magazine. In many companies there have been extremely supportive individuals who perceived the value of the unit to the supply of qualified and committed personnel to the industry as well as understanding the value to the degree provision at North London and to the personal and intellectual development of the participants.

The key experience of the unit has been the placement. It has proved essential to establish clearly the nature and scope of the project that students would undertake on placement with host companies in advance, in order to ensure satisfaction to all three parties: student, company and academic staff responsible for the unit. Examples of the projects undertaken on placement include the picture research for a major literary reference work, the layout of a number of pages for a major national magazine and conducting an interview and laying out the subsequent article for an in-house magazine. In addition to the specific project undertaken students were introduced to the range of activities of the host company as a form of work-based learning on the key issues of publishing indicated above.

The assessment of the unit also focuses on the placement and was designed to assess the skills and knowledge which the unit aims to develop. Assessment takes the form of a log of work-based learning, constituting 40 per cent of the mark, and a written project – based on the placement – together with an oral presentation to the group on the project, constituting the remaining 60 per cent. The knowledges and capabilities which the unit aims to teach and assess are: an understanding of the roles and responsibilities within the publishing industry and how they interrelate an ability to discern the particular constraints within which publishing operates, and a basic knowledge of the technical specifications and terminology used in the industry. The personal transferable skills which the unit seeks to develop are: an ability to plan and organise effectively (with an awareness of the demanding schedules of publishing houses), the ability to manage a range of tasks to deadlines and the ability to work effectively, both independently and as part of a team (including the requisite communication skills).

The unit has facilitated entry to publishing as a career for those with the necessary capabilities and commitment. A number of students have continued to work part time for publishers after the end of the placement and this has provided further valuable experience. One graduate of the unit is working for the Women's Press after a spell at *The Guardian*, while two others have obtained jobs at Stonehart Leisure Magazines. Three currently have offers to undertake the Diploma in Publishing and Printing Studies at the London School of Printing and thereby full professional training. It should be remembered that the unit is not vocational training for the publishing industry but a single unit option within an English degree that affords insight into the material production of forms of contemporary literature as part of the academic study of English literature. It develops such knowledge and understanding through work-based learning as well as classroom study. Additionally, it provides students with a context closely related to their academic area of study in which to practise the transferability of the capabilities nurtured by the humanities and in which to consider their personal and career development. Some, but by no means all, may be contemplating careers in publishing. It is as important that it enables some to identify that such activity is not for them, as that it is an excellent route into publishing for the enthusiastic graduate.

Chapter 14

Oral History for Undergraduates: A Skills Perspective

Kathryn Castle

Introduction

Transferable skills in the humanities is a topic that has generated a good deal of attention and, at times, debate. In the recent revalidation of the history degree at my own university the history group made explicit its view on the complementary relationship of specialist and generic skills.

History at the University of North London aims to develop . . . the historical and general skills which will empower the student as a historian, as a trained professional, and as a self-informed and confident member of the wider community. These include conceptual and analytical powers, the ability to work independently and cooperatively, an increased competence in written and oral expression and the self-confidence which will enable them to seek, secure and hold employment beyond their University years.[1]

The incorporation of a skills-based approach to the teaching of history is demonstrated by the provision of methodological units in each semester at preliminary level. In these units students are introduced to the nature of the discipline and its social applications, while emphasis is given to the development of oral competence, skills of quantitative analysis, the opportunities of humanities IT and evaluation of visual sources.

In addition each history module now includes in its aims and learning outcomes a clear statement of the particular skills (oral, aural or written) associated with the unit and reflected in the assessment pattern. In short, historians have accepted the need to think more clearly about the relationship between historical and general skills, to ensure that undergraduate units address both aspects of learning and to highlight in course materials the interactive and complementary relationship which exists between the two.

Part of the continuing revision of the history curriculum has been the introduction of areas of study which particularly rely on oral sources. Five years ago I introduced, and others have subsequently taught to preliminary level students, the unit 'Women in History'. An important component of the assessment for this unit is the oral history exercise. The rationale for introducing this mode of assessment suggests how a subject area can simultaneously respond to the changing boundaries of a discipline and answer the needs of its student body. Collecting evidence about women's lives is a critical part of expanding what we know of the past, and at the same time involves students in a stimulating and rewarding task.[2]

The expansion of academic interest in this field corresponds with the profile of a student population diverse in age, experience and ethnic origins and keen to take an active part in history as a 'hands-on' activity. Part of this process is a desire on the part of many entrants to retrieve hitherto neglected areas of study, which serves both as a confirmation of identity and the expansion of historical resources. This in turn democratises the practice of history, removing distinctions between teacher and learner and transforming the group into cooperative practitioners – demystifying the role of the working historian and implicitly empowering the individual.[3]

Finally it should be noted that sending students out to conduct an oral history interview can be seen as one way of removing the boundary walls between the university and society at large. Moving the agenda of history out into the community confirms a necessary interdependency between the historian in action and the individual in society. History 'comes to life' in more than one sense. Oral history, in this way, is a part of the redefinition of student 'learning', which identifies the resource base as expansive and interactive. The stress on a proactive approach is both energising for the learner and a signal, early in their course of study, that an independence of mind and practice is an integral part of historical training and self-development. It has been satisfying to note that a number of students return to oral history as the primary source for extended third-year projects, often with excellent results.[4]

The project

The oral history component is a distinctive and important part of the Women in History unit. This is a semester-based module of 15 weeks' duration, which introduces students to the theory and practice of women's history. Writing and analytical skills are developed in a documentary exercise and short essay, while oral and associated skills are paramount in the group discussion and oral history assignment. In a unit which emphasises and values the importance of prior experience as well as academic sources it would be unlikely that oral competence would be confined to the interview itself. Lively sessions of small group discussion over a variety of topics in the weeks preceding the interview are invaluable in building a shared commitment and in exploring methodological and practical concerns.

In semester-based courses time is short, however, and part of the first meeting is set aside to introduce the oral history. For most students, and even if interviewing has been part of their work experience, this is a new and for some quite daunting proposition. The tutor needs to explain clearly what is expected and set the students thinking about the necessary forward planning. The choice of interviewee is crucial and much discussion will centre on how to identify a person whose life experiences might illuminate areas of interest. A key concern is the identification of possibilities to explore continuity and change in women's lives. From this starting point the group is encouraged to identify issues which might be productively addressed: motherhood, sexuality, family relations, work, education, political roles and the impact of external events, such as the Second World War or the women's movement. Students are advised to contact and coopt their interviewee as soon as possible, acknowledging that the holidays (Christmas or Easter) might be appropriate times to conduct an interview.

The assignment in its final assessed form is no longer than 1500–2000 words. This represents not a literal transcript, but rather a summary of the substance of the interview, highlighting the main areas covered, the most interesting information gleaned and the most appropriate direct quotations. Students are encouraged also to hand in a tape of the interview if possible and, if they wish, a full transcript, although only the summary will provide one-third of the unit mark. The oral histories of past years are kept as a useful resource for current students to consult and may one day form the basis of a valuable collection.

Having identified a potential subject and been advised of the form in which findings will be presented, students are directed toward source books on the theory and practice of oral history. Guidelines from the Oral History Society are made available which provide useful pointers. The tutor also presents a framework in which to approach the exercise and the nature of the oral skills involved. Key points for reflection include:

- the distinction between a conversation and an interview;
- the relationship of interviewer to interviewee, how to establish a rapport in the exchange, issues of familiarity and distance, how to ask open-ended questions;
- thinking out the questions well in advance and maintaining an awareness of the priorities in information sought;
- maintaining an awareness of the needs of women's history – filling in the gaps of secondary works, answering neglected questions, challenging the view of traditional sources and texts;
- establishing if the interviewee requires the questions in advance or wishes anonymity, the possible rejection of a tape recorder.

Midway into the unit, in week six or seven, students are asked to update the tutor on their progress toward the interview in week ten. Setting the interview date before the end of the unit allows the group to report back their findings, even if not in fully finished form. This is useful in allowing time for reflection and reinforcing the sense of a group as well as individual project.

The outcome and conclusions

The results have been consistently good. Even initially weak and unconfident students perform well. All acknowledge enjoying the process and express a consciousness of achievement. In some cases there is clearly a personal element of satisfaction as well. Participants who interview members of their own families or close acquaintances often report a new perspective on the lives of those they thought they knew well. The interview situation can liberate women to talk of experiences and events hidden from their families as well as from the historian. Increased respect, interest in and affection for the interviewee is often noted. As is so often the case in women's oral histories, the distancing of the traditional sociological or historical interview model is superceded by a sense of liberation and pleasure in talking about, sharing and legitimising areas of women's lives.[5]

In the follow-up sessions the group is encouraged to think about the variety of skills which they have brought to the assignment and developed within it. They have exercised responsibility over the choice of interviewee, the setting of questions, the retrieval of information and the parameters of the discourse. It has been their ability in establishing contact, showing sensitivity to developments in the interview, adapting and asking supplementary questions and distinguishing between areas to pursue or abandon which has facilitated a successful outcome to the exchange. These are invaluable skills, transferable to innumerable public and private arenas. Those employers who decry the ability of graduates to communicate effectively and show flexible, creative and rapid strategic thinking would be well advised to look closely at the increased confidence and competence of students who undertake such tasks.

Alongside the confidence that emerges from individual achievement there is a sense of contributing to a valuable academic and social activity. Not only are the participants expanding the knowledge-base of women's history, but they are part of the process that legitimises women's experience and recognises its validity as part of the story of the past. Interviewees express surprise and appreciation that their experiences are of interest to a student of history and that the 'university' has a relevance to their own lives. These bridges are invaluable in redefining the learning community and establishing its resources in a wider context.

The benefits of the exercise are undeniable, both in terms of the student experience and the quality of work produced. Its value as an arena of transferable skills can be summarised as follows.

- Students take great pride in the work produced, the quality of which is often outstanding.
- Students show clear evidence of having acquired what they view as a new skill – the ability to conduct an interview successfully, collate and interpret the results.
- Students view the exercise as a product of their own initiative, and see themselves as the 'active historian', rather than the passive interpreter of secondary works.
- Students believe that they are contributing in a socially useful way to the body of knowledge in a critical area of history, and view the information as relevant to their own lives.
- The exercise increases self-confidence, verbal skills, strategic thinking, attention to detail, critical faculties and social awareness.

For graduates of the 1990s and beyond, who will need not only a knowledge-base but also the skills to gain and sustain employment, this experience is a useful introduction to the possibilities of a history curriculum where the skills of the discipline are clearly interactive with the needs of the learner. Historians are well placed to adapt their teaching strategies to reflect a responsibility for student experience and the value-added element in a student's progress through a course of study. In the case of oral history, students, the community, potential employers and history all benefit from the results.

Notes

1. 'History Definitive Document', course document produced by the University of North London, 1994, p. 3.
2. Deidre Beddoe (1987), *Discovering Women's History*, Pandora, London, p. 11.
3. Paul Thompson (1978), *The Voice of the Past*, Oxford University Press, Oxford, pp. 2, 7–8.
4. Topics have included generational changes in Asian families, local history studies, memories of the Second World War in London and testing the 'reality' of George Orwell's vision of Britain in the 1930s.
5. For a useful discussion of the feminist approach to oral history see S Gluck and D Patai (1991), *Women's Words: The feminist practice of oral history*, Routledge, London.

Chapter 15

Drawing in Interior Design:
The Portfolio
Susan Williamson

Introduction

A contemporary profile of interior design

The term 'interior designer' conjures up for most people an image of a stylishly dressed, snappish woman doing expensive and judgemental things with the interior of your home.

Perpetrated with full colour visuals through Sunday supplement features on gracious living and consumer durables, this image has lived on in fantasy and in parallel with the less well-known reality of the path that the majority of professional interior designers in fact follow.

Interior designers are trained through a difficult, lengthy and both project- and theoretically-based education starting with BTEC, a foundation course or work experience, following on to an HND in one of the three-dimensional design fields or a BA (Hons) in the same. This culminates for an increasing number with postgraduate education in interior design or architecture, as interior designers today graduate to work in a number of fields. These include architecture, film/television, the theatre, museum/exhibition/installation, domestic design, furniture and crafts, the commercial sector (the chief destination for interior designers, including as it does design for retail, shopping centres, hospitality and leisure, offices, industrial locations, shopfitting, product and packaging), graphics, design for the public sector (community-related fields such as health and correction facilities, libraries, public housing) and design research.

The term 'interior design' is constantly under attack for its difficult combination of misleading specificity and bland generality. Various alternate descriptions for the field include 'interior architecture', 'three-dimensional design', and the simple 'design'. 'Interior decoration' is a term familiar to the public but avoided by interior designers, who view interior decoration as an area for two-dimensional exploration of soft furnishings and surface decoration. At the same time interior designers do daily battle with architects, product and graphic designers over territorial infringements. The current definition of interior design is broad and equally broadly contentious: design which has as its focus the experience of the human senses; design at a small scale; design for use, touch and spectacle; design which may equally be outside or inside, or interestingly the threshold that links the two; the space between buildings; design as palimpsest, or for the next layer on the heavily redrawn sheet that is the reused building space of today.

With the confusion surrounding the public perception of interior design, the profession's own inability to define itself to the satisfaction of its members, and the ever-broadening fields that interior designers now colonise, it is hardly surprising that this perplexity extends to interior design education.

Changes in interior design education

Academic institutions and the workplace

Traditionally, interior design in the UK was taught as an art-based subject. Making the transition slowly from short courses in fine finishes, crafts, furnishings and business practice that characterised training for interior decoration (a training which continued on the job), interior design courses took on a more theoretical approach which married the project problem solving of interior decoration to a philosophical base that sprang from architecture. In Europe interior design has been largely a by-product of architecture; in North America the field has had a long three-part grounding in business, technology and small-scale commercial design. It was the boom of the 1980s that gave interior design in the UK its first real public prominence as an important 'added value' to commerce, and consequently opened up for the first time a serious debate about the role of industrial links and credibility in the market-place for interior design education.

The Interior Design BA (Hons) course in the School of Architecture and Interior Design, University of North London has made the series of transitions of educational expectation that many other such courses have been forced to make in the last ten years. It became increasingly apparent that interior design students needed the experience the workplace could offer to offset and complement the theoretical and art base of academic training. One of our answers has been to institute an industrial placement element to the curriculum, rendering it a sandwich course and stretching it to a total of three and a half years. (The industrial placement element, taken nationally and internationally, falls between the second and final year.) The sandwich course was begun during the tail end of the economic boom period, in the expectation that the design-led retail peak of that market would provide abundant opportunity for young designers to gain professional experience during their education. In fact the last four years have been as disastrously lean for those students as for the trained professionals in our field: with the retail, service and construction sector having been hit hard by the recession, the traditional source of employment for interior designers contracted enormously.

Competing academic and industrial pressures

In spite of the recession our design students have each gained a placement every year (most have had more than one) during their seven-month industrial break. We attribute this to heroic efforts on the part of staff members, a widespread marketing campaign, the recognition that students must broaden their target expectations to include a very wide range of possible design fields, careful preparation prior to placement and, most importantly, months of worry, strain and chasing of opportunities by the students themselves.

A yearly battle is waged between the placement tutor trying to prepare students for professional interviews by helping them profile themselves through CVs and portfolios of work that will appeal to a commercial market, and the rest of the academic staff who are frustrated by the students' evident preoccupation with these preparations to the detriment of their studies as they bastardise their academic portfolios to suit anticipated interviews. Nevertheless, in spite of the best efforts of both placement tutor and the students, their portfolios are far too often seen as unrealistically academic when viewed by potential employers.

Our course relies on the goodwill and commitment of the design profession to offer students this valuable industrial experience. And so, after one particularly telling letter from a potential employer:

'having interviewed three [students] we have reluctantly decided that we are unable to offer a placement to any of them. We regret having to make this decision, as the Practice has an established commitment to helping with the training of architecture students and we wish to extend this to include interior design. Unfortunately we felt that the students on offer fell short of the standard we would customarily expect students we employ to attain, particularly in the area of graphic presentation.'

and the consequent chagrin on the part of the three academically impeccable students who had been interviewed for the above position, an idea was born.

In my current position as Course Coordinator, with years of experience in the industry, I felt that the apparent chasm dividing academic expectation of 'the portfolio' and industrial expectation of it was based more on ignorance than on reality. It was also felt that students and the course itself would benefit from having placement and other industrial representatives involved in the academic discussion that surrounds the design portfolio.

The portfolio as a bridge between education and workplace

The design portfolio carries a heavy burden of responsibility, representing variously a body of work, a personal profile, a piece of academic propaganda and a series of visually explicit pieces of both two- and three-dimensional work. It forms the primary method of holistic appraisal of a designer's progress as a student and professional value as a potential employee. The methods of representation and communication used to transmit design propositions which make up the design portfolio are the subject of debate both in the academic forum and the workplace.

The Enterprise in Higher Education (EHE) scheme for 1993–4 offered us an opportunity through a funded Curriculum Development Project to look at these media and methods of communication of design intent and (measured and freehand two- and three-dimensional drawings, analytical and observational drawing, computer-aided drawing and animation, collage and mixed media rendering, photography and video, modelling and prototyping) their role as the bridge between education and experience. Having carried out a series of developmental meetings with studio staff to establish the main areas of concern to be addressed by the project and the central aims and objectives to be achieved, the writer set up a formal year-long project which through its very discipline was to attempt to avoid that ghost at the academic feast: the prospect of vigorous undocumented debate leading to nothing more than the pub.

Composition of EHE Curriculum Development Members Project

A number of professional designers (all of whom had had some form of previous contact with our students and their portfolios) were invited from various design fields to participate in our study. A three-part Steering Committee was set up of these representatives, students of all levels and representative studio design staff and subject tutors (teaching technology, contextual studies, art and design representation and professional practice). The industry representatives brought experience in such diverse fields as design for film and television, theatre, retail, exhibition/ museum, hospitality, large architectural projects, domestic design and design for the public sector, complementing the professional backgrounds of the teaching staff (most of whom are also in practice).

The Steering Committee meetings took place in a variety of settings, including the year studios, the off-site graduate degree show and the end-of-year school-wide exhibition. Agendas were set and followed, minutes distributed, written feedback requested and received, creating an unprecedently well-documented study into the role of representation and communication in interior design.

Terms of the Project

Common understanding

Essential to the success of the project was to establish a common understanding of the issues. These were agreed to be the following.

1. That 'drawing' in interior design should be taken to include all methods of representation and communication of design intent, both two- and three-dimensional, and including freehand, orthographic, measured and technical drawings; analytical and diagrammatic explorations; perspectives, both sketch and measured, line or rendered; single and mixed media, collage; photographs, video and film; modelling, both conceptual and representational; prototyping and crafting; information technology/computer-aided design (IT/CAD); verbal and graphic presentation; performance and installation.
2. That while employers are chiefly looking for evidence of skilling in the form of a practical design-led 'quick and professional' response as shown in effective two- and three-dimensional drawing skills, academic concerns centre on the developmental, experimental, analytical and qualitative nature of methods of representation and communication.
3. That the semester of industrial placement falls at a point in the curriculum where students have not yet achieved a skills and competence base that is fully in line with the needs of the marketplace.
4. That it is equally in the interests of teachers, students and design professionals that students attain basic skills and competences in the craft of their profession, without detracting from or shortening the developmental experience of a design education.

5. That there is common ground in the educational aims and outcomes of the placement experience and in continuing interface and support between design educational bodies and the design industry.

By updating the definition of 'drawing' into one that encompassed all contemporary means of design expression, the hurdle of perceived practical banality (on the part of the employers) and the necessity for proper skilling in all mentioned fields (directed at the academic institution) was overcome.

By identifying the semester of industrial placement as the overlap period to be tested, all three groups had a vested interest in the success of the project's outcome.

And by assuming common interests on the part of all three groups prior to debate, an atmosphere of symbiosis rather that of rivalry removed the usual impenetrable surface layer of suspicion which has so frequently prevented fruitful discussion in the past on this topic.

Areas of project examination

The following areas were singled out for examination:

1. competition among and mutual exclusivity of representational teaching approaches;
2. 'common currency' of representation in student studio year groups leading to a lack of breadth and a lack of understanding of more holistic methods and media;
3. intermediate-level portfolio at the time of the industrial semester did not demonstrate full range of representational skills owing to curricular and timetable constraints;
4. ambition and philosophy of the course, in concentrating on the *process* of individual design development, did not allow for full representational and *detail* development, which thus led to insufficient experience in the detailing, materials manipulation and representation necessary for employability of students in the profession;
5. that the placement semester (between the second and third year) frequently discouraged students from experimental and developmental work and made it difficult for them to reintegrate into the course curriculum and pace upon their return for the final year.

By admitting that there were problems on all fronts – teachers, students and employers – defensiveness of position was lessened and areas for attention identified surprisingly easily.

Substance of project

The following decisions were made and carried out over the process of the project.

1. The curriculum was examined in detail through students' presentations, debates in front of exhibited works, tours of the studios and written feedback from all participants.
2. Workshops were held on the following themes:
   a) 'image-a-day' had preliminary-level students examine the language of means of representation and communication through the graphic deconstruction of the work of certain designers and architects. The students presented their exhibition to the Steering Committee for discussion.
   b) 'The detail pyramid' series of group workshops, conceived by the project leader and designed and carried out by one of the industry representatives on the Steering Committee, involved intermediate-level students in day-long group trials of research, analysis, deconstruction and proposed further development of non-standard and standard professional detailing (and brought the new area of 'fax detailing' to the attention of the Committee). The students and the design professional involved presented the results of the workshop to the Committee for debate.
   c) 'Professional presentation' workshops for intermediate-level students run by design professionals introduced students to new possibilities of professional graphic representation, and helped focus them on further development of their portfolios in anticipation of forthcoming interviews for placement positions. The results were presented to and discussed by the Committee.
   d) 'Project management' day-long workshops for intermediate-level students, conceived by the project leader and developed by the design professional who carried them out, gave students a practical taste of the requirements of the industry, through group projects which had as their outcome each day a different 'package' of researched, specified, drawn and presented design proposals based on partial information of an existing project. This series of workshops was particularly popular, and students presented their achievements to the Committee for discussion.

Project outcomes

Practical outcomes of the project have in the year following included the addition of these workshops into the curriculum of the course and the designation in our course of 1994–5 as 'the year of the portfolio'. Particular areas of study will include professional detailing, advanced perspective, professional visualisation methodology, multimedia portfolio methodology, the portfolio 'before, during and after placement' and the theory of the design portfolio. Funding from EHE has been extended to address this new focus, and industry representatives on the Steering Committee will 'close the circle' of the project by devising and teaching several workshops within this theme.

For 1995–6 several significant alterations to the course structure have been validated. These changes are as a direct result of, among other generators, the original EHE project 'Drawing in Interior Design' and thus:

1. the design projects in studio will become less prescriptive and wider ranging, and through lengthening and doubling up of modules now allow for both 'quick response' workshops and projects within the design curriculum and for the logical development of design projects to detail stage with the full representational exploration demanded by the profession and needed for student skilling and competences;
2. the principal means of assessment of both design and representational skills and competences will be through the academic portfolio;
3. technology, representation and communication, history and professional practice components of the course will be further integrated into the studio, leading to better rounded design exploration and less fragmented portfolios.

The course team is also presently re-examining the role, timing and nature of industrial placement within the curriculum with a view to its possible positioning at the end of the course and/or to the extending of placement to a year to include a semester of exchange abroad.

Conclusion

The EHE Curriculum Development Project 'Drawing in Interior Design' was considered very successful by all concerned. It was unprecedented: a disciplined forum for a very specialised debate about one of the essential 'truths' of the changing field of interior design, which had more than merely discussion and process. It had meaningful and welcome outcomes and a longlasting effect on the nature of teaching and the curriculum of the BA (Hons) course in Interior Design at the University of North London.

Incidentally, the potential employer whose dampening letter had spurred us into action became one of the most helpful members of the Steering Committee, and his final feedback comments conclude this chapter.

'The reviews and discussions have already produced a positive response within the School to address this issue and should reflect favourably on students' work, particularly those going out into professional release and having to adapt rapidly to real working situations.'

Chapter 16

Developing Grammatical Skills for Language Learners

Nicole McBride and Karen Seago

Changes in higher education over the last decade have affected every aspect of the academic environment. Nowhere has this been more strongly evident than in the shift away from the conventional A level student to a much wider spectrum of students who come to university through a variety of entry routes. Skills and competences acquired outside the academic framework can now be accepted as equivalent qualifications to those gained in school and this has led to an increased intake of mature and non-traditional entry students.

The transformation of the student population has inevitably introduced changes in course delivery and an exploration of new methods of learning and teaching. Out of this has evolved an overall philosophy of broadening and enhancing students' experience during their university courses. With the Enterprise in Higher Education (EHE) initiative this development was further related to the world outside the university. It directed attention to skills and competences acquired in the academic context which could be transferred into non-academic environments. The extended opportunities available through wider access to higher education are thus carried through to greater equality of employment opportunities for university graduates.

156

The ethos of equality of access has brought about changes in course design which have been particularly apparent in language study, where the offer has been extended to degree courses in which the language can be studied from scratch[1] or non-academic acquisition can be formalised. Thus an increasing proportion of students embark on undergraduate language learning, entering with different abilities and varied needs and attending various modes of study; they may have relevant experiential learning yet, as mature or non-standard entry language students, they may never have studied a language formally; their first language is not necessarily English and their experience in language learning can be that of a non-European language with a very different linguistic structure.

In addition, language teaching in schools in the past two decades has tended to shift emphasis from a widely used grammar–translation approach to a focus on communication skills.[2] These factors explain the low awareness of grammar among traditional and non-traditional students, who cannot exercise 'the kind of conscious control over language which enables them to see through language in a systematic way'.[3] The result is that most students need to learn about grammatical categories and functions in order to support language teaching and learning. Various reports and guidelines from the Department of Education and Science have attempted to return to a more balanced approach and this is also reflected in the national core curriculum.

THE A TO Z OF GRAMMAR project was set up to provide a flexible learning resource for language beginners and returners.[4] Its aims were to enhance grammatical awareness and thereby maximise real access to language learning and subsequent progress, not just for a few students but for a diverse and increasingly multicultural group. It gives to a wider range of individuals than has traditionally been the case genuine support to start or revive a language at higher education level or to take it to degree level.

As a learning development project concerned with language acquisition skills THE A TO Z OF GRAMMAR contributes to the curriculum, to learning and teaching methods, to assessment and to educational support systems.

A familiarity with key grammatical functions and concepts (eg object, accusative, gender, tenses) is a necessary aspect of the Modern Languages curriculum, particularly for specialist linguists. In the current context of declining resources, which have led both to an increase in class sizes and economies in contact time, this subject component was identified as one which could benefit from becoming more student centred and from being managed by students in their own time, as independent study. This determined the type of medium we chose. It had to be stimulating, widely accessible and allow a self-paced approach so as to encourage students to develop a positive attitude towards grammar and linguistic awareness in general. In addition, it had to provide a neutral environment in which 'trivial' queries about any aspect of grammar can be explored (and repeated) without fear of embarrassment. The chosen resource needed to fulfil a tutorial role by guiding the students towards appropriate practice and providing immediate feedback. Furthermore the range of language provision available in most HE institutions requires the management of large numbers of students and pathways. Efficiency can be increased through producing learning material which is available on open access. A computer-based resource fulfils all these requirements with the added advantage that it can be easily updated.

THE A TO Z OF GRAMMAR

THE A TO Z OF GRAMMAR is a multilingual resource focusing on French, German, Italian, Spanish and English as a Foreign Language (EFL) available both in language laboratories and on open-access to a wide spectrum of primarily ab initio and intermediate language learners. It consists of a computer-based corpus of fundamental grammatical functions and concepts regularly used in the teaching and learning of a foreign language and includes definitions, explanations and examples.[5] Interactive questions and linked exercises at every step of the process allow immediate transfer from the theoretical level to practical application.[6] The program provides practice and feedback as well as opportunities for more formal self-assessment.

Not having been exposed to much grammatical description, learners are usually intimidated by the terminology. They find it difficult to relate to categories and functions which cannot be immediately recognised in the structure of English, where there is no apparent difference, for example, between a noun used as subject or as object. The program therefore provides a short introduction to each concept, which attempts to give a working definition of, for example, what an 'object' or 'gender' is. The approach is contrastive, taking English structure as the basis for explanation and comparison but pointing towards different practices in other languages.

A more detailed treatment follows in each of the five language pathways, explaining the specific usage of the concept as it applies to the chosen language. The design caters for different levels of knowledge by allowing learners to determine whether they wish to stay on the 'top level' for an overview, or whether they wish to investigate particular aspects in more detail. These 'excursions' are available as expansions which unfold when the user clicks on a clearly signalled *active* text area or a button. Multilingual learners have the opportunity of following up cross-references between languages, to reinforce a particular aspect through comparison of identical usage or to become aware of possible interferences through opposing structures in two languages. Such links are also available between grammatical concepts, showing the inter-

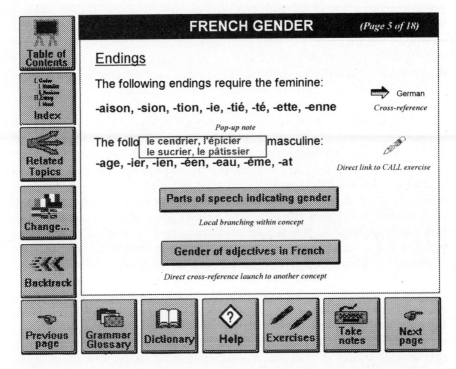

Figure 16.1 *Language-specific screen with navigation and learning tools.*

related nature of many structures; this is further supported by the 'related topics' function, pointing users towards other aspects which have a bearing on the topic and which it would be useful for them to investigate. This integrative approach facilitates the development of a broader insight into language structure by linking up apparently disparate elements.

On every screen the program presents several options and students determine which one they are going to follow when they interact with THE A TO Z OF GRAMMAR. For instance, in Figure 16.1, students can click on any of the endings for a number of examples in the target language demonstrating the point in question to appear in a little overlay window (see 'pop-up' note: le cendrier . . .). They also have the opportunity to compare the morphology of endings (and gender) in German, or they can decide to 'jump' to two other areas where gender plays a crucial role by clicking on the labelled buttons in the text window. Alternatively they may wish to reinforce their retention of feminine and masculine endings by clicking on the pencil to do a linked exercise practising this.

After launching a computer-assisted language learning (CALL) application students are automatically returned to their 'original' screen in

THE A TO Z OF GRAMMAR on finishing the exercise. They can then resume a linear reading of the topic or they may wish to check in the index for subtopics within gender. If they come upon a use of terminology they are not familiar with they can click on the grammar glossary for a short explanation; similarly the dictionary provides a translation for unfamiliar words in the target language examples. Thus students are necessarily in charge of their learning, yet the program also provides educational support and this is by nature integrative with the rest of the teaching/ learning sequence. It actively supports class-based language activities and enables learners to follow up grammatical queries independently, as often or as rarely as their own linguistic background requires. The tool itself is a multifaceted resource. It provides an integrative platform – a framework[7] – for a number of CALL applications and a range of learning aids which can support language investigations and self-directed study. Learners have immediate access on the screen to dictionaries, grammatical glossary, indexes and a notepad as well as the facility via several buttons to move in a linear or non-linear way between 'pages' or to retrace their steps.[8]

THE A TO Z OF GRAMMAR addresses primarily cognitive skills which are content specific and aim to develop the understanding of grammatical concepts and the acquisition of language structure. At the same time, because language acts as a delivery vehicle for other disciplines, the resource addresses generic abilities central to literacy in higher education and as such exercises skills much sought after by employers. Developing insights into the structures of a foreign language not only strengthens receptive and productive skills in that language but can transfer into the first language and lead to improved performance in activities such as reading and writing. The multilingual content fosters a comparative approach to language structures and an awareness of linguistic diversity; at the same time it promotes recognition and acceptance of differences and relativities in other academic areas and activities. With this background students can develop the ability to recognise and value divergent perspectives in a variety of contexts.

Students become more actively involved in and responsible for their own development and as a result less dependent on staff to manage their learning: they initiate their own queries and they decide on the appropriate procedure to complete these queries. This is a form of 'empowerment' which prepares them for a changing work environment.[9] Current feedback from students using trial versions has confirmed that they appreciate being in control of their learning strategies within the program and that they are aware of these benefits. The program also enhances the development of a range of generic abilities such as:

• objective setting (defining a query to answer);

- problem solving (deciding on how, where, how often to retrieve relevant information, relating it to other knowledge, developing personal understanding and assessing oneself);
- organisation and independence (managing within a specific time-scale);
- adapting to changes (using an electronic media).

In giving students significant control over their learning strategy[10] – while providing a structured framework for the less secure learners[11] – the approach enhances individual responsibility and is inherently self-affirming.

All these skills are used in the effective planning, gathering and handling of information in other academic or non-academic situations. They are clearly relevant to future study and to the world of work and should help graduates address some of the demands of their professional careers. Subsidiary core skills developed by THE A TO Z OF GRAMMAR are dependent on the medium: the new technology, and in particular hypertext, used in this project. Users are exposed to the Windows interface and different applications, ie hypertext, wordprocessing facilities and various CALL packages. They become acquainted with accessing and retrieving information and researching with the support of electronic dictionaries, indexes and glossaries. These abilities are easily transferred to new applications and different contexts.

In conclusion, THE A TO Z OF GRAMMAR develops not only grammatical skills and subject-specific cognitive skills for language learners but also personal competences transferable to other situations and circumstances and generic skills related to IT literacy. The change in both method and medium that it represents signals a new approach to learning for students and staff;[12] a shift from a communicative programme – delivered in class with the teachers as facilitators – to a mode of study which is computer based and interactive and which foregrounds self-directed learning.

Notes

1. The same opportunity of starting a language at ab initio level is open to qualified 19-year-old entrants, who may not have had the opportunity to study a particular language at school.
2. For further discussion see Metcalfe, P (1992) CALL, 'The foreign language undergraduate and the teaching of grammar: A linguistic and political battlefield', RECALL 7, Nov.
3. Carter, R (1990) 'The new grammar teaching', Chapter 5 in Carter, R (ed.), Knowledge about Language and the Curriculum, Hodder & Stoughton, London, p.119.
4. It started in 1992–3 as a curriculum development project funded by the EHE.
5. It has been developed in the hypertext authoring system GUIDE (by software developer OWL International, Washington, USA).

6. Interactive questions involve learners in a process of deduction by inviting them to draw their own conclusions from the material presented so far; opening up hidden text gives the 'answer', thus providing feedback on whether their deductions were correct or not.

7. In doing so it avoids the pitfalls in self-access of 'the discreteness of the presentation of the grammatical topics' (Glencross, M (1993) 'Grammar and CALL: A review of current practice in some French language programs', RECALL 8, May, p. 21) and facilitates access.

8. The book metaphor is used as a presentation strategy to support the computer novice. For further information on the program see McBride, N and Seago, K 'THE A TO Z OF GRAMMAR: An integrated CALL project', in CALL Journal, Autumn/Winter, 1995.

9. See the article in the Careers section of the *Guardian* when F Colquhoun points out that 'the workplace demands a new kind of employee and a new kind of manager who own and manage their destinies', *Guardian*, 14 January 1995, p. 3.

10. Piloting suggests that support is required to assist students initially in managing learning which does not necessarily conform to their expectations of studying towards a degree.

11. Learners can follow a linear sequence and limit themselves to the constantly displayed top level of THE A TO Z OF GRAMMAR.

12. For staff this involves investigating and implementing new ways of managing, facilitating and assessing learning. The project has delivered considerable returns in terms of staff development. It has allowed teachers from different languages and areas to work effectively towards the design and implementation of new *enabling* learning environments for their students, to produce quality participative learning resources while grappling with the necessary developments of their IT literacy skills.

Conclusion
Alison Assiter

The book has offered the reader a snapshot of the kinds of project developed in one institution – the University of North London – designed to facilitate the development of students' transferable skills. As Harold Silver has pointed out in his Foreword to the collection, the University of North London is by no means unique in the direction it has taken. Its focus on profiling is distinctive (although Oxford Brookes University has developed in a similar fashion on this topic); but it shares with most universities – old and new – which have been in receipt of EHE funding the experience of attempting to enhance or facilitate the articulation of students' skills.

The focusing on 'skills development', moreover, is not unique to the UK. Outside of the UK context similar changes are taking place. For example Australia and New Zealand are developing competence-based systems of education. A number of writers have noted, however, that the Australian approach is more holistic than that adopted by, for example, the National Council for Vocational Qualifications (NCVQ). In the EC context, for instance in Germany, the Fachhochschule (which are broadly vocational universities) offer integrated university–company education programmes. These are developed by an association of the Fachhochschule, the German Industry and Trade Board and the German Employers Association. Work-based programmes appear to be partly 'competence

163

based', although the concept is very broadly characterised, and the work of Habermas is influential in the characterisation of the programmes.

There remain, no doubt, many unanswered questions about the concept of a 'transferable skill'. One of these will be about the relationship between the kinds of skills development outlined above and the competence approach taken by the NCVQ. We have not dealt in any detail with the NCVQ in this book, partly because there has been extensive coverage of the topic elsewhere, and partly because there is no agreement among the contributors to the volume about this question. Some have reservations about the reading of competence offered by the NCVQ, while other would be happy to deploy the NCVQ approach.

A further question which may occur to some readers concerns the notion of 'transferability' itself. We cannot take it for granted that skills developed in one social or cognitive context will automatically transfer to another context. Instead, as David Bridges has argued, it may be important that we encourage the development of the 'meta-competence' of 'transferring'. Bridges quotes Fleming, for whom,

'transferring skills. . . are. . . the metaskills, the second-order skills which enable one to select, adapt, adjust and apply one's other skills to different situations, across different social contexts and. . . across different cognitive domains.'

Bridges' approach is borne out by Brown's emphasis on 'metacompetence: the generic ability which provides the resources to develop competence in specific situations'.

One such model of skills development is that of the 'expert practitioner' (see, for example, Crebert, 1995). According to Crebert an expert practitioner possesses a number of different sets of skills, all coordinated and activated in practice by strategic thinking, or the 'ability to recognise the appropriateness of particular decision-making strategies for particular situations or under certain conditions'. Strategic thinking is itself grounded in critical self-reflection and the ability to 'bring past experience to bear on current action'. (See also Cervero, 1992.)

Such a model might be represented like this:

University/workplace

↓

An expert/practitioner

↓

Strategic thinking skills

↓

Procedural/conceptual/organisational/social skills

Crucial in this model is the notion of the learner learning how to reflect critically on his or her learning processes in various contexts, and the differences and similarities between them.

Building on the above, one Australian academic, Marginson, has developed the following model of the 'expert practitoner':

Expert practitioner

↓

Critical self-reflection

↓

Capacity to move between different viewpoints, languages, systems of knowledge

↓

Awareness of context

↓

Learning how to learn

In other words, on this model, the specific skills required are generic, and include an awareness of context, the capacity to move between viewpoints, self-reflection and learning how to learn (Marginson, 1994).

This model resonates with the criticism of the behavioural approach to competence developed by (amongst others) Burgoyne (1993), Holmes and Joyce (1993) and Assiter (1993). Holmes and Joyce have argued that a modified notion of competence, incorporating the ability to discuss issues and reflect critically upon them, would be a useful development. It also coheres with psychological research which suggests that most of the evidence for the transfer of skills comes from studies which have attempted to teach 'thinking abilities'. (Although some psychologists have found little evidence of transfer of particular skills, even if the domains are similar. For a useful discussion of some of the psychological literature, see Green, 1994.)

The above model, then, sees skills, particularly critical thinking skills or abilities, developing in a disciplinary or a workplace context. The model might also incorporate other specific skills; these too would grow out of the subject context.

An alternative model of skills/capability development, however, is the Alverno model. Alverno College is a women's college in Milwaukee, USA. Like the Australian approach, elaborated above, Alverno takes the development of critical thinking to be crucial (see, for example, Alverno

College, 1984). In the Alverno model a list of desirable skills or abilities and values was first drawn up, including communication and analysis. Lecturers from all disciplines across the institution agreed that each one was important for all students to develop; they were each perceived to be important both for all discipline-based learning and for subsequent employment. The next step, for them, was to agree common definitions of the concepts, by abstracting shared features of, for example, communication across disciplinary contexts. Thus they were involved in a process which directly contradicts the claim made by Tony Becher, that there are discipline-specific cultures that it may not be possible to transcend; and that, for example, communication understood in the context of physics is incommensurable with 'communication' understood from the perspective of philosophy (see Becher, 1989, 1994).

Staff in Alverno now believe that each of their separately listed abilities are independently essential to the learning of academic disciplines. In other words, they believe that it is as important for students to acquire the skills of communication as it is for them to learn biology or history. They set out, therefore, to help students understand the analytic and communicative conventions within particular disciplinary boundaries. At the early stages of development of each ability, Alverno faculty work to develop each ability separately. Each ability is broken down into a sequence of six levels: the first four are 'generalised' levels required of all students, and the last two are specialised subject-specific levels. In the case of analysis, the six levels are as follows:

1. observes accurately;
2. makes justifiable inferences;
3. relates parts or elements in patterns;
4. integrates patterns into whole systems;
5. compares and tests frameworks in their discipline;
6. integrates frameworks into a professional synthesis.

The first four of these are general across all disciplines; the last two are discipline specific.

In the case of each ability students are invited to bring, at the outset of each programme, examples of self-assessments of their ability levels. For example, in the case of communication, the student is asked to provide examples of ability in writing, speaking, reading and listening, each in a particular format. Students are given one lecture demonstration on the self-assessment of each ability.

Alverno has undertaken systematic research on the transferability of the abilities gained in the college context to the workplace, and this research reveals a very high level of transferability.

The Alverno model suggests that certain pre-identified capabilities are taught at first in a generic fashion. At 'higher' stages the skills are integrated into the disciplinary context. The model, then, would look something like this:

	A	B	C	D
Level 1 Generic abilities				
Subjects				
Level 2 Generic abilities				
Subjects				
Level 3 Subjects and abilities				
Integrated				

Each of these models conceives skill broadly, in a fashion that resonates with Boyatzis' definition of competence as 'an underlying characteristic of a person which results in effective action and/or superior performance in a job' (Boyatzis, 1982, p. 61). Underlying characteristics can include natures, skills, traits, aspects of one's self-image or social role, or a body of knowledge. Indeed, it has a strong affinity, as I have argued elsewhere (Assiter, 1993) with the medieval 'guild' model of knowledge. The apprentice in the guild was supposed to acquire knowledge 'informed by reason', knowledge that involved a consideration of the value of alternative ends and a judgement as to which of the various alternatives was the best end or aim to pursue. The broad approach to transferable skills outlined in both of the above models of skill development has similar aims.

The chapters in this book demonstrate both models in operation: transferable skills, including 'thinking' skills, have, on the whole, been developing in a discipline or specific work-based context. However, the developments outlined above have formed part of an institutional strategy (akin, in some respects to the Alverno practice) and, as many of the contribbutors have indicated, their work has drawn on good practice from elsewhere.

References

Alverno College (1984) *Analysis and Communication at Alverno: An approach to critical thinking*, Alverno Production, Milwaukee, Wisconsin, USA.

Assiter, A (1993) 'Skills and knowledge: Epistemological models underlying difference approached to teaching and learning', *Reflections on Higher Education*, 5, July, pp. 110–124.

Becher, Tony (1989) *Academic Tribes and Territories*, Open University Press, Buckingham.

Becher, Tony (1994) 'The Significance of Disciplinary Differences', *Studies in Higher Education*, 19, 2, pp. 153–63.

Boyatzis, R (1982) *The Competent Manager*, Wiley, New York.

Burgoyne, J (1993) 'The Competence Movement: Issues, stakeholders and prospects', *Personnel Review*, 22, 6.

Cervero, R M (1992) 'Professional Practice, Learning and Continuing Education: An integrated perspective', *International Journal of Lifelong Education*, 12, 2, pp. 91–101, esp. p. 96.

Crebert, Gay (1995) 'Links between Higher Education and Industry: Workbased learning programmes in Australia – practices and issues', Academic Staff Development Unit, Queensland University of Technology. Paper presented at conference on International Issues in Work-based Learning, GEC Management Centre, April 1995.

Fleming, D (1991) 'The Concept of Meta-competence', *Competence and Assessment*, 16, p. 10.

Green, Alison (1994) 'A Psychological Approach to Identifying Transferable Skills and Transfer Skills', in D Bridges (ed.) *Transferable Skills in Higher Education*, University of East Anglia Press, Norwich.

Holmes, Len and Joyce, Paul (1993) 'Rescuing the Useful Concept of Managerial Competence: From outcomes back to process', *Personnel Review*, 22, 6, pp. 37–52.

Marginson, Simon (1995) 'Competency-based Education: A compilation of views'. Paper presented to the Australian Education Union, January 1995.

The Contributors

Unless otherwise stated, the contributors are based at the University of North London.

Stuart Allen is Senior Lecturer in Accounting in the Business School and a Member of the Institute of Chartered Accountants of Scotland. He previously worked in both the private and public sectors.

Alison Assiter is Director of the Enterprise in Higher Education programme. She also directs a project on educational guidance and teaches on the Humanities programme. She has written a number of books on feminist theory, most recently *Enlightened Women: Modernist Feminism in a Postmodern Age*. She has also edited *Using Records of Achievement in Higher Education*, published by Kogan Page.

Sue Bailey is Senior Lecturer in Consumer Studies and Placement Tutor for BSc (Hons) Food and Consumer Studies students. Her research interests are factors affecting food choices of older adolescents and transferable skills and work placement learning strategies.

George Blount is involved in the industrial liaison function within the Business School. He had a career in sales and many years commercial experience before joining the Business School.

Anne Brockbank is Head of School (Management and Professional). Her current research and consultancy interests include management development, interpersonal skills, women in management and the learning process. She is author of *Life Choices* and has recently contributed to *Women in Organisations*.

Kathryn Castle is Principal Lecturer in History and Programme Director for Caribbean Studies, South Asian Studies and History. Her main research interests are in the areas of social and cultural history, particularly popular culture. She is currently finishing a book on the representation of non-Europeans in British history textbooks and children's periodicals between 1890 and 1940.

169

Adrienne Clarke is Principal Lecturer in European Studies and Director of International Affairs in the Business School. Her main research and teaching interests lie in the area of European social policy, particularly relating to women's participation in the labour market, and in developing students' study skills.

Paul Corrigan is Head of Quality at the London Borough of Islington. His current research interest is primarily the relationship between the local state and civil society and the way in which service delivery interacts with democratic experience in the locality. He has written a number of books, including *Schooling the Smash Street Kids*, *Social Work Practice under Capitalism* (with Peter Leonard) and *Striking Out* and *The Cultural Production of Labour* (with Mike Hayes and Paul Joyce).

Tim Dodd was until recently a senior lecturer in Behavioural Science and Personnel Management in the Business School. His research interests include work group behaviour, employee participation and Japanese and British management practices and he has written about the nature and results of Japanese management practices in the UK. He was the tutor in charge of placements of the BA Business Studies degree from 1989 to 1994.

Marta Dueñas-Tancred is a Senior Lecturer in Spanish and Latin American Studies. She is subject tutor for the year abroad and also works as an interpreter for English companies dealing with Spanish business. She is working on a study of urban speech in Latin America and has written articles for *Nueva Revista de Fologia Hispanica* and *Estudios Centroamericanos*.

Mike Hayes is Director of the Applied Social Research Unit and Principal Lecturer in the School of Policy Studies, Politics and Social Research. His main interests include qualitative methodology, trade union research and the politics of the labour movement. He has written *Striking Out* and *The Cultural Development of Labour* with Paul Corrigan and Paul Joyce.

Len Holmes is currently Faculty Coordinator for Enterprise in Higher Education in the Business School, where he also teaches organisational and employment studies. He worked as a manager in the hotel and catering industry, then as a training practitioner, before entering teaching in higher education. He is currently doing PhD research on management ideology and managerial identity.

Sue Johnstone is senior lecturer in the Business School and the course tutor for BA Business Studies. She is interested in trade union law, equal opportunities and media law. She has written articles on employment and trade union law.

Trevor Joscelyne is Head of Higher Education and Access Development; he was formerly Head of the School of Literary and Media Studies. His main areas of interest and research are curriculum and learning development with reference to the enablement of student learning. He has written on Shakespeare and seventeenth-century poetry, and in contemporary theatre.

Professor Paul Joyce is the Stanley Kalms Reader in Strategic Management and Business Ethics in the Business School. His main interests are in the strategic management of public services, local economic development and business ethics. He is currently engaged in researching strategic management and business ethics. He has written *Striking Out* and *The Cultural Development of Labour* with Paul Corrigan and Mike Hayes.

Nicole McBride is a member of THE A TO Z OF GRAMMAR project team and lecturer in the School of Languages and European Studies. She teaches French, Linguistics and IT at the University of North London. Previously she taught French at Essex, and worked for two years at the Bureau pour L'Ensignement de la Langue et de la Civilisation Français (BELC), Paris. She has published course materials and reference books in language learning and teaching and has been involved in CALL for the past ten years.

Professor Kenneth MacKinnon is Principal Lecturer in Film Studies. He is co-translator (with George Valamvanos) of Vangelis Katsanis' *The Successors* and *An Anthology of Modern Greek One-Act Plays*, and he has written extensively on Greek tragedy and film.

Barbara Page is Course Tutor for the Science and Engineering foundation course and EHE Coordinator for the Science, Computing and Engineering Faculty. Most of her working life has been concerned with bringing industry and education together, and her present area of research interest is in the teaching of practical chemistry in schools.

Karen Seago is a member of THE A TO Z OF GRAMMAR project team and a lecturer in the School of Languages and European Studies. She teaches German Language, Literature and Theory at the University of North London. Prior to that she taught German Language and Interpreting at Salford, and she has been involved in CALL for the past five years.

Harold Silver is currently visiting professor at the University of Plymouth and Nene College. He was formerly Professor of Education and Social History, University of London, and Principal, Bulmershe College, Reading. He has published many books, such as *An Educational War on Poverty* (with Pamela Silver), *A Higher Education* (a history of the CNAA), and *Good Schools, Effective Schools*, and is at present working with Pamela Silver on *Students: changing campus roles*.

David Taylor is Director of the MA Scheme in Environmental and Social Studies and Academic Links Coordinator. He researches and publishes in the area of social policy, citizenship and social identity. He is a member of the Editorial Collective of the journal, *Critical Social Policy*. From 1991–3 he was Faculty Coordinator of the Enterprise in Higher Education initiative.

Frances Tomlinson is Principal Lecturer in Organisational Behaviour in the Business School. Her teaching and research interests include cross-cultural management, group processes and team working, and gender in organisations. Recent research projects in which she has been involved include studies of women's employment in publishing and retail management and of Equal Opportunities in the higher education curriculum.

Val Walcott works in the field of industrial liaison and was employed in the University of North London at the time of the Enterprise in Higher Education project.

Ruth Watson is the Enterprise in Higher Education Student/Employer Links Coordinator. Her main interest is working directly with students to foster a critical awareness of their own personal development and potential.

Inge Weber-Newth is Senior Lecturer, subject tutor and year abroad tutor for German in the School of Languages and European Studies. Her teaching covers a variety of aspects of German: language, contemporary affairs, literature and culture. Her research interests are in migration studies, ethnicity and identity.

Susan Williamson is Course Coordinator of the Interior Design Degree in the School of Architecture and Interior Design. She is Principal of Genius WR Ltd, a multidisciplinary design consultancy in London. Her main interests lie in multidisciplinary design, the North–South design dialogue and design by non-designers, and the social psychology of design.

Nick Winstanley is Senior Lecturer in Business Policy in the Business School. He had a career in marketing and general management before entering the academic world. His consultancy interests include: corporate strategy, business start-ups, staff development, recruitment and team building.

Glossary of Abbreviations

AGCAS	Association of Graduate Careers Advisors
AGR	Association of Graduate Recruiters
BAAF	BA in Accounting and Finance
BABS	BA in Business Studies
BTEC	Business and Technician Education Council
CAD	computer-aided design
CALL	computer-assisted language learning
CBI	Confederation of British Industry
CIHE	Council for Industry and Higher Education
CNAA	Council for National Academic Awards
COMBUS	Combined Studies in Business (BA degree course)
CPD	Continuing Professional Development
DE	Department for Education
DES	Department of Education and Science
EFL	English as a Foreign Language
EHE	Enterprise in Higher Education
ERASMUS	European Community Action Scheme for the Mobility of Students
ESRC	Economic and Social Research Council
FE	further education
HE	higher education
HEC	Higher Education for Capability
HND	Higher National Diploma

IMS	Institute of Management Studies
IT	information technology
NAB	National Advisory Board for Public Sector Higher Education
NATFHE	National Association of Teachers in Further and Higher Education
NCC	National Curriculum Council
NCVQ	National Council for Vocational Qualifications
NFER	National Foundation for Educational Researchers
NIACE	National Institute for Adult Continuing Education
NVQ	National Vocational Qualification
NUS	National Union of Students
PNL	Polytechnic of North London
PSQ	personal skills and qualities
ROA	Record of Achievement
RSA	Royal Society of Arts
SCED	Standing Conference on Education Development
SRHE	Society for Research into Higher Education
SSS	Applied Social Science degree scheme
TA	Training Agency
TEC	Training and Enterprise Council
TEED	Training, Enterprise and Education Directorate
UCL	University College London
UGC	University Grants Committee